'Everything is extraordinary . . . especially this book. Cole Morton has piled human story upon story, each one a shining, particular gem, each one with its own unique character like the funny, foolish, brilliant, brave individuals whose stories they are, each one uniquely didactic, each one universal. The book's ending is the best I've read in a long time.'

Claire Gilbert, author of *I, Julian*

'Cole Moreton's remarkable skill to is to show us that when we pay attention in this life, attention pays us back. His stories catch glimpses of the luminosity, intimacies and significance of human experience, all reminding us that, when it comes to meaning, love is the only metaphor worthy of our pursuit. His fresh honesty never fails to open windows in the soul.'

Mark Oakley, Dean at St John's College, Cambridge

'Cole Moreton hosts a gathering of extraordinary people, some acknowledged everywhere, others whose extraordinariness goes unnoticed. He hosts with generosity, wisdom, candour, and an enviable eye for detail. He also gets thrown out of a car by Archbishop Desmond Tutu and ejected from Violet Kray's funeral aged fifteen, so there's bravery too.'

Richard Coles, author of *The Madness of Grief*

'Everything is extraordinary and few things are more extraordinary than the remarkable encounters recorded in this book. Here are some of the most fascinating people of our time all gathered in one place. This has to be the ultimate dinner party!'

Gyles Brandreth

'I've never read a book quite like this one – Cole Moreton has a campfire storyteller's knack for setting the scene as if we are actually in the room with Scarlet, Clive, or Zahra . . . (or briefly in a car with Desmond); he has a therapist's genius for calling forth the deeper truths about the people he interviews; and a memoirist's facility that helps us learn deeply too about the author (without being self-indulgent). More than that, *Everything is Extraordinary* lives up to its title – not just by being a rare and beautiful thing, but by reflecting to the reader the wonder most of us struggle to see in ourselves.'

Gareth Higgins, author of *How Not to be Afraid*

Also by Cole Moreton

Hungry for Home
My Father Was a Hero
Is God Still an Englishman?
The Boy Who Gave His Heart Away
The Light Keeper

Everything is Extraordinary

*True stories about how we
live, love and pay attention*

Cole Moreton

HODDER &
STOUGHTON

First published in Great Britain in 2023 by Hodder & Stoughton
An Hachette UK Company

2

A CIP catalogue record for this title is available from the British Library

Hardback ISBN 978 1 399 80037 2
ebook ISBN 978 1 399 80038 9

Typeset in Sabon by Hewer Text UK Ltd, Edinburgh
Printed and bound in Great Britain by Clays Ltd, Elcograf S.p.A.

Hodder & Stoughton policy is to use papers that are natural, renewable and recyclable
products and made from wood grown in sustainable forests. The logging and
manufacturing processes are expected to conform to the environmental regulations of
the country of origin.

Hodder & Stoughton Ltd
Carmelite House
50 Victoria Embankment
London EC4Y 0DZ

www.hodderfaith.com

Contents

LEARNING TO FLY

'You wanna fly, you got to give up
the shit that weighs you down.'
Toni Morrison

Preface

'Attention is the rarest and purest form of generosity.'
Simone Weil

Hello. Thank you for picking up this book of stories, every one of which is true. They're all about meetings with remarkable women and men, some of them famous or infamous and some of them not. I think we're all remarkable actually, but more of that in a moment. The title is taken from words that were said about the Australian writer and broadcaster Clive James and the way he saw the world in his final days. I work as an interviewer for national newspapers and radio, so I had the privilege of going to see Clive at his home in Cambridge during a strange but precious time in his life. He had announced in print that he was dying of cancer and would not see out the winter, prompting full and gratifying tributes from friends and admirers, but the doctors were managing to keep him alive for longer than expected. There was extra time to reflect on his life, loves, regrets and joys and that's what he did as we sat together one long summer afternoon. Clive was in pain and grieving for the years he would miss of course and he raged against the dying of the light, as you would expect from a man who had punched out prose like a prizefighter all his life; yet he was also full of a new grace and gratitude for being allowed to stay in that light for a while longer. He saw resonant beauty in even the smallest things. Every moment was potentially precious, because there were so few left. You can read about what it was like to be in the room with him in the story that bears his name. Clive's experience became even more intense towards the end, as his daughter Claerwen later told the writer Rachel Cooke, a family friend, who quoted her in the *Guardian* as saying: 'His world had shrunk to this room, and that terrace. He never went anywhere, he saw almost nobody, he could eat almost nothing – and yet, every aspect of his life was filled with meaning. The fact that there was an apple on that tree; whether it was rainy or sunny. Everything was extraordinary.'

Those words ring true with me. I have chosen them as my title as a way to suggest some of the things I'm trying to explore in these stories, including the power of connection and the possibility that we might see how extraordinary the ordinary really is. Every story stands alone, but together I hope they also add up to a reflection on life as learned from these encounters, a meditation on what it means to be human and how we might do it well. How to live, love and pay attention. How to connect with each other, with ourselves, with the world around us and the divine, if we believe in that.

Not that this is a self-help book. I can barely help myself sometimes.

I just go around asking questions, watching reactions, listening to the answers and telling stories, because I do believe we are at our best when we open up to each other. That's when the unexpected happens, things are revealed and we get a few clues to what life might be all about. Sometimes there are glimpses of glory in the smile of a friend or the sight of a bird on the wing, as described in the chapter called Kes. Sometimes we have nothing to go on but rumours, passed on by people like Clive who are further ahead down the road than us and willing to share, if we are willing to listen. And that's really what this book is about. Sharing.

Listening. Seeing and being seen. Learning from each other. Daring to open up, daring to hold each other's gaze. Daring to care.

The stories feature women and men who are wealthy beyond all dreams and others who have almost nothing in material terms but are rich in other ways. Each person has something valuable to pass on, whether by accident or design and whether they know it or not. We all do. I grew up in a diverse community of loving, creative working-class people who were led to believe our voices were worthless. That was not true. We were burning with stories, even if nobody wanted to know. The old man who'd secretly been a Spitfire pilot, the mother with a head full of Caribbean memories, the lonely boy who thrashed a guitar in his bedroom, the little girl next door who saw colours in his music as it came through the walls they had tales to tell and insights to pass on. We all have, even if they're buried deep down inside, waiting for someone to care.

Each of us is of equal worth, so I try to take everyone in these stories at face value as a broken, beautiful human: whether that's Scarlett the Hollywood superstar hiding out in a hotel bar in Manhattan on the day her marriage disintegrates or Tiger the fallen hero, unable to stop himself telling the truth; or Zahra, who crossed the Channel at dawn one Christmas morning on an overladen rubber boat at the end of a 7,000-mile journey that sounds like an ancient folk tale. We will be travelling the world together in these tales, from the East London of my childhood to the glamour of the Upper East Side and from the warmth of the West Bank to the wild seas raging in the far west of Ireland, with the wind and sky pressing in, each place becoming part of the conversation.

I hope you will take pleasure in the way the stories are told, because they are primarily written to entertain and for the joy of the telling and hearing. Read them out loud if you like, the people on the bus won't mind. Share them. Enjoy them. Listen to me reading some of them as you go, on the podcast that inspired this book called 'Can We Talk?'. Whatever you do, thank you for spending time with them. The French philosopher Simone Weil once wrote to thank a friend for reading her writing and said: 'Attention is the rarest and purest form of generosity.' She was right. I'm grateful to the men and women in these stories who allowed me to sit down with them and I'm also very grateful to you, for paying attention to what I have written. Let me know what you think, when you're ready. As Desmond Tutu says in the chapter that expresses so much of what I'm trying to say here: 'I can't be a human being on my lonesome. I wouldn't know what to do.'

Life is better when we share, so shall we make a start?

*   *   *

LIVING

'I can't be a human being on my lonesome.'
Desmond Tutu

Scarlett

Fifteen minutes is all you get with Hollywood stars. Fifteen minutes in a neutral room, in the company of a publicist or two. It's hard to make any kind of connection in that time and New York is a very long way to go for fifteen minutes with someone, however famous she is. Still, I found myself thousands of miles from home at the start of 2017, in a winterbound city with a strange energy. I was drawn to Trump Tower, where cops with machine guns stood at the door, surrounded by steel barriers and black Humvees, and the crowds waited, as if the new president might turn up at any time. There was no sign of him though, so after a while I walked on by to my hotel, which turned out to be owned by Trump too. It was as if everywhere you might go and everything you might do was dominated by the Donald. Half a million people had been on the streets of Manhattan the day before, stopping traffic and yelling out their rage. The ghost of the protest still haunted the hotel entrance, where the doormen looked wary.

Up in my room I dropped my bags and fell back on the bed, listening to the thrum of the city come through the walls and the triple-glazed window, which didn't open.

I was high in the sky, sealed in a box, thinking about the opening scene of a movie called *Lost in Translation*: a long, still shot of a young woman lying on her side, on a bed in a hotel room very like this one, with the same tuneless city song playing. We see her legs, her backside in yellow cotton, her torso with a blue vest top riding up at the waist. We're invited to see her as perfect. Young, healthy, gorgeous.

When that scene was shot, Scarlett Johansson was eighteen years old. Now, as I was about to meet her, she was thirty-two and one of the most famous humans on the planet. Her movies had made more than five billion dollars at the box office at that point, thanks to *The Horse Whisperer*, *The Avengers* and *The Jungle Book*. She was said to be worth more than $100 million in her own right.

'Hello?'

The door opened unexpectedly, there was a flurry of apologies and a woman entered. Reception had given me the room early, there were still things to do. The housekeeper was busy, distracted and no doubt on a tight schedule; but I'd watched a Tom Hanks movie on the plane over, in which his character asked the name of anyone he came across, to connect with them. I couldn't resist trying.

'Renata,' she said briskly.

'What did you make of the protests yesterday?'

Her lips pursed, she didn't want to answer, this wasn't a movie, but she did anyway: 'The guests were angry.'

'What about?'

'They couldn't get into the hotel.'

'Okay,' I said as she disappeared into the bathroom with a basket of toiletries, 'but what do you think of it all, personally?'

Renata stopped what she was doing, came back out and stood looking at me, weighing up whether to say anything. I saw her name on her badge now, black letters on white plastic against a black uniform. She made eye contact and my pulse quickened. For a moment, we weren't just strangers. She wasn't just servicing my room and getting out of there. I guessed Renata was in her early thirties like Scarlett but on a low wage, on a zero hours contract, under a lot of pressure. Still, she stopped.

'They are right, I think. He's not my president.'

She'd heard the chanting at the rallies, heard about the wall he was building.

'He hates us. That's what it sounds like to me anyway.' She spoke in a low voice, not wanting to be overheard. 'I'm from Puerto Rico. He doesn't even know it's American.'

I asked if she was scared. Renata smoothed the front of her black skirt with both palms, picked up her basket and prepared to leave. 'This is our country.'

I nodded.

She smiled. 'Have a good day.'

'You too, Renata. You too.'

*　　　*　　　*

The phone buzzed with a message to say the location for the interview had been changed and the time put back: 'Scarlett will meet you at the Carlyle Hotel on the Upper East Side at 4 p.m.' I could walk through the fresh January cold, up through the spine of Manhattan, then across Central Park. Usually, I love New York. The taste of possibility in the air is intoxicating. That day, though, there was a sense that what was coming, for the city and for America, might not be great.

Maybe there was a similar sense back in 1930, when the Carlyle Hotel was built by Moses Ginsberg, an immigrant from Poland who'd made a fortune. Not even the financial crash could stop Moses putting up a forty-storey hotel and apartment tower in a grand art deco style; but two years later he was forced to sell at auction for a fraction of the price he wanted. Now, long after Moses, the Carlyle was still one of the most famous hotels in New York, an intimidating sight. It took guts just to walk in the door.

*   *   *

I was looking for The Gallery – 'an exquisite, private retreat for refined dining' according to the hotel – inspired by the Topkapi Palace in Turkey. Deep red wallpapers, banquettes made with antique kilims and red-fringed velvet chairs. I felt more than a little out of place. And Scarlett was late. Very late. She had the right to be, of course. Only Michael Caine, Johnny Depp and Tom Cruise were ahead of her in box office power. She didn't have to do this, or anything else, ever. The one thing in my favour was that she had a place around the corner somewhere, having grown up nearby.

Her mum was a film fan and sometime producer, of Ashkenazi Jewish descent, partly from Poland like old Moses Ginsberg. Her father was a Danish architect. Her school was in Greenwich Village, but Scarlett wanted to be Judy Garland and her mum was willing to indulge that fantasy, taking her to auditions. There was real talent in her, too. She made her film debut at the age of nine, but it was *Lost in Translation* that won her first acclaim. It's a beautiful, elegant, poignant film about the relationship between her character, Charlotte – a young wife lost and lonely in Japan – and Bill Murray's much older, fading movie star, also adrift in the neon land-scape. I felt a bit like that myself, sitting there in the half-light of the Carlyle Hotel's deepest, plushest rooms. We'd come to New York as a family a few years before, but the old life seemed to be fracturing and I was afraid of what might come next. It was good to be away, but I didn't belong here. And I was nervous, as ever before an interview. Even a bit feverish.

'Hey, how ya doing?'

Heads turned at the unmistakeable voice of Scarlett Johansson: deep and smoky, with a New York twang. She appeared as if by stealth, like Black Widow but in a bulky green parka with a fur-lined hood. This wasn't a superhero, nor even a movie star, but a real person, shrugging off her rain-soaked coat and handing it to the concierge, who signalled that he recognised her with nothing more than a flicker of the eyelids.

I'd expected more from the moment, to be honest. She was routinely described as one of the most attractive humans on earth, so I had thought she would sweep in like Marilyn Monroe, wafting sensual appeal and causing men and women on all sides to swoon. Not a bit of it. Scarlett was brisk, businesslike, ordinary. Nervous or stern, I wasn't sure which. She was wearing glasses with thick black rims. Her hair was cut in a boyish flick. Her ears glittered with multiple tiny silver rings. She wore black jeans and a simple black leotard top. The only thing showy about her was a pair of Doc Marten boots, artfully splattered with paint of many colours. She looked small, funky, elegant in a punky, art school kind of way. Totally unlike the vast electronic billboard of her in superhero mode I'd seen in Times Square on the way here, over a hundred feet high. And there'd been smaller versions all along my walking route, advertising her new film. I told her this and she laughed. 'Yeah, I see those everywhere. That's good, I guess.'

How did it feel to be surrounded by images of herself like that? And more to the point, when everybody in the world knew her face, her body, her voice and had an idea how she might behave, how did she hold on to a sense of her self?

'You mean your own truth?'

She smiled and frowned at the same time, perhaps a little surprised to get to this stuff so quickly, but I didn't have time to waste. She'd be gone in fifteen minutes. Half an hour, if I could get her talking and fend off the PR.

Wait though, where was the PR? There was no sign of them, surprisingly, as Scarlett settled down into one of those deep velvet chairs.

'I'm private of course, I'm a private person and I live pretty low-key, as much as I can. And living in New York aids that, very much so. I grew up here, I was born and raised here, so I can scurry around the streets like any other city rat, pretty much.'

Her friend David Bowie had come to live in New York and found it the best place in the world to hide in plain sight. 'I used to see Bowie at the Bowery Ballroom, he was just taking in new music like any other person and New York is great for that. It's got a great attitude, the city. But yeah, I guess that once you accept that some of those pre-conceived ideas that people have about you are truths about yourself, you stop fighting that a bit.'

Which ones? 'I don't know. Perhaps that I'm an outspoken person . . .'

Right on cue, the people at the next table shut her up by speaking loudly to each other about something neither of us caught properly. She looked down at my recorder. 'Do you wanna move?'

'I'm okay,' I said, not wanting to waste a moment. 'But I do want to be sure it catches your voice. Can we shuffle up a bit?'

'Sure,' she said, getting closer, but I noted a nervous cough.

She didn't know me. I'd been vetted by the PR company working for the new movie, but I could have had any number of strange issues, so I did my best to be relaxed, to give her personal space, to not get intense. We were knee to knee now, alone together here. Nobody else was coming. Scarlett was still thinking about how she kept things real.

'Becoming a mother has been the most humbling experience.'

That was a platitude, sure, but I could see how giving birth to a daughter would change the priorities and awareness of a person who'd been the centre of attention since childhood, the star and the talent in every scene. Her daughter Rose was three years old. Rose's father was a French magazine editor and entrepreneur called Romain Dauriac, who apparently hadn't been able to speak any English when he met Scarlett. Things moved fast and they were married a month after Rose was born.

'Going to therapy, being curious about yourself. Remaining curious about my job. Living in New York City. Having everyday encounters, living my life. That helps me connect all of the different parts of myself to one person. It's an ongoing trip.'

Being a New Yorker was obviously a big deal to her. I'd read that Romain was keen to live in Paris full-time with Rose, while Scarlett travelled for work. That would be a challenge, surely? But I was all too aware of the need to ask about her new movie, before we ran out of time. Once again she was wearing a skin-tight catsuit to fight bad guys, so I asked how she felt about the way women in superhero movies were always being squeezed into unlikely fighting costumes? 'I don't know, that's hard to say, because I work alongside guys that wear skin-tight leather leotards, you know, for work!' She was talking about *The Avengers*, including Chris Evans as Captain America. 'And basically you spend all day making jokes about, like, their various codpiece sizes.'

She was funny. Scarlett also had the rare ability to move through combat scenes like someone who could actually fight, but was that right? 'Part of the challenge of doing these jobs is overcoming my own fears of confrontation and my own doubts about my physical ability,' she said. 'I don't have the sixteen years of training that my amazing stunt double Heidi Moneymaker has. That's her real name. She's my shadow. You learn to fight the same way, you mirror each other. It's a kind of ballet.'

I chanced my arm with a tease. Could she take me down, if she wanted to?

'Are you trying to start a fight with me? With this tea cup in my hand?'

I thought I'd gone too far, that she was offended or unsettled, but Scarlett smiled again and shook her head. 'No, I'm good. I'm a peaceful person.'

She spoke like a character in a Woody Allen movie, which of course she had been several times: *Match Point*, *Scoop* and the rather better *Vicky Cristina Barcelona*. Woody Allen said of her: 'It's very hard to be extra witty around a sexually overwhelming, beautiful young woman who is wittier than you are.' In retrospect that sounds a bit creepy. There was definitely something about her that made people go all gooey though; and if I'm absolutely honest with you it was happening to me, just a little bit, there and then. Scarlett Johansson was laughing and smiling and touching my knee for emphasis, just as a friendly, tactile person might do. But the vain male part of my brain – the inner chimp if you like – was beginning to believe somehow, against all the evidence, that this was terrific, we were getting on well, this was a kind of date.

I do know that wasn't true. I knew it then. If there had been time for an internal dialogue, I would have told my inner chimp to shut up. Unfortunately, as I tried to get a grip and looked down at my notes for a change, the first question I saw was from my fifteen-year-old daughter, who loved Scarlett. I had promised to ask this question, so I had to:

'What is it like to know that almost everyone you meet fancies you?'

'Ha! Nice. Yeah. That's definitely a question from a fifteen-year-old,' she said kindly. 'Certainly, for as many people I meet who fancy me – that's a very English way of saying it – there is another half of people just completely think, "Who does this person think she is?" You know what I mean?'

Not really, but I was being careful what I said. I wondered, how had she survived in the horrendously sexist world of the movies?

'The whole world is like that. It's true in any industry. Hell, it's true walking down the street. I remember walking down the street in New York, nobody knew who the hell I was, being fifteen or sixteen years old and having guys catcall, you know? I was in Washington Square Park at some parade with my girlfriends and all of us got groped by the same creepy person that walked past. We had to find a bunch of police officers and find this guy and make a report.' Did they have him arrested? 'Yeah.'

I suppose I was asking about this to show that I wanted to be on her side, but also because the rise of Trump had caused her to speak up. 'It's time to get personal,' she'd told a rally in Washington at which half a million women had gathered to protest against the incoming president's behaviour and policies. He wanted to close family planning clinics; she had talked about going to one of them for help and advice at the age of fifteen. 'Normally, I don't feel I need to talk to people about my intimate care,' she told me now. 'Obviously. Even more so, I'm private because everything I say is pulled apart in a million different ways and repurposed. But at this point, I don't care. At this point, I feel that if I can share my story and make an impact, that's way more valuable to me than preserving the remnants of privacy.' Scarlett was even thinking of running for office. 'I am just sick of it. I am sick of this conversation being in the mouths of politicians: what I'm going to do with my body, whether my friends and I are going to be valued equal to our male friends and family. It feels so archaic.'

She had found something at the protests that was otherwise missing in her life. 'This amazing feeling of sisterhood, this like-mindedness, this camaraderie. Men and women alike. It was incredibly uplifting and powerful.'

A common enemy connects us. A common cause can inspire us.

'I'm standing up for myself. I'm standing up for my sister and my daughter, my mum and my friends. All of us. I've had it.'

*   *   *

The daughter who had wanted me to ask that question about being fancied is a triplet. I mentioned that to Scarlett, because she is a twin. 'I'm very close to Hunter. He's my bro, he's the best. He's working in a bar downtown part time. So I go and hassle him in there. "Bartender! Bartender!" ' We were way over time now, at least in my head, but this had turned into more of a chat about life. I expected it to end at any moment, but instead Scarlett went deeper.

'One thing that's really interesting, that I've realised in the past couple of years, is that I have never actually been alone. I really have always been with somebody.' She meant from the womb. 'And in those first moments of life, even just the spark of it, having somebody else there must affect one, right? Because of it, I'm learning now how to be alone, just with myself. But it's challenging. It's a funny thing. It doesn't mean I haven't felt alone at times, or lonely, but I'm just realising that I've always had this other half out there.'

Learning to be alone is a challenge for anyone, even more so with a twin, but those words must have had an extra, huge personal significance to her that day, because of things that were going on in her life. I would only find out about them later. 'Being a twin affects all your life. I notice in my intimate relationships, I've chosen people as a result of not wanting to feel alone, or trying to fill some kind of space. It affects you, always.'

We talked about how she and Romain had homes in New York and Paris but would have to choose a base when their daughter Rose started school. 'Yeah, then we'll all be in one place. She's two-and-a-half now, so we're at that wonderful stage. She sings a lot. She's always been pretty good at sleeping. I like to sleep too.'

I thought of the young Scarlett sleeping on that bed in Japan, forever a teenager in a beautiful movie. There were so many images of her out there, so many ways for people to see her and think they knew her. Then I thought of Scarlett the mother, sleeping with a child by her side. And I thought of this happy family, skipping from New York to Paris and back; but then again, the vain chimp in my brain started to chatter. We'd been together now for much more than an hour. Fifteen minutes was a distant memory. Was she too shy to stop and leave? Surely not. As the afternoon slipped into evening, I started to think that maybe she'd stayed to talk because she liked me. That was a seductively flattering thought. She was a film star, THE film star. Half the people in the world would have killed to be in that room, drinking with Scarlett, shooting the breeze, on a kind of date. There's that word again. Was this turning into a date? Even just a little bit?

No, of course it wasn't. What a stupid idea. How deluded men can be, even when we know better. This was an entirely professional conversation between two people who both knew how to create a feeling of intimacy quickly: an interviewer, whose livelihood depended upon it; and an actor who was in the habit of creating winsome characters at the same time as keeping herself to herself. That was all. I was sure of it, until the next day.

* * *

I woke up to find social media full of stories about Scarlett Johansson, who had been photographed in public the previous day without her wedding ring. This was taken as a sign that her marriage was over. My editor emailed from London: 'What did you do?!!' It was a joke, of course; an ironic, blokey take on the idea Scarlett might have met me and realised that her life with Romain was empty, she needed a real man, like me. I told him not to be daft. Then I started thinking. Was she wearing a wedding ring? I didn't know. I hadn't noticed. I'd been a bit dazzled. But I did remember what she'd said: 'I've chosen people as a result of not wanting to feel alone, or trying to fill some kind of space.'

Had I missed the true meaning of those words, on the day? Yeah, but how could I have known them? She had given me every reason to believe she was happy with her life and her lover. She'd created a moment that felt authentic, but wasn't the whole truth. Brilliant. So here's the big reveal: Scarlett Johansson is a terrific actor. Still, even allowing for the antics of my inner chimp, it did feel like we'd shared a few, brief moments of connection: talking about life and laughing like friends. So what had just happened?

Maybe it was the knowledge she could end our conversation at any time and just walk away that made it work for her. Maybe it was the same with Renata, when she was kind enough to stop and talk. Life must be a lot less comfortable when you clean the rooms in a Trump hotel than when you're worth $100 million, but maybe the desire for connection is the same. The desire to be heard. The need to look someone in the eye and feel understood, if only for a moment. It's worth chasing after. It's worth stopping for when you find it, because whoever you are, the work can sometimes feel too hard, the schedule too fierce, the crowds too overwhelming, the noise and the rage too much to handle. Whether you live in Trump City or not. We all feel a bit lost in translation sometimes. Adrift in a strange land. And when that happens, we need to be kind to ourselves, take time out. Rest. If you feel like you're performing, then make like Bowie and Scarlett and stop the show. Turn off the lights. If you feel like you need to be alone, then be alone. And if you feel like you need human contact then find it, any way you can, even – in a safe way – with a stranger. When she did leave, after so unexpectedly long, Scarlett Johansson rose and pulled on her parka, opened her arms for a light hug and said: 'That was lovely.'

Did she mean it? I hope so. I think so. I think she may have been feeling the hurt in her life that day and seized the unexpected chance to escape all that for an hour or two, taking time out in a quiet, elegant, private, familiar place where nobody was watching, to chat with someone who might have seemed easy to talk to, giving him the illusion of intimacy but at the same time protecting herself. Finding company, on a day when she may have felt really alone. And there's our first lesson: sometimes you just need to hide away, and that really is okay.

*   *   *

Tiger

We're waiting for Tiger. Dozens of us. Men with cameras for heads; women clutching clipboards to their chests; sports presenters with powdered noses; and me with a notebook and a voice recorder. Two actually, for safety. And a crowd of wide-eyed kids, waiting with their mothers and fathers and guardians, in the corridor of the W Hotel. We've all been here for hours, waiting for our promised moments with the man.

Waiting for the legend.

Waiting for the greatest golfer of all time, who is so much more than a golfer, so much more than a multimillionaire who hits a tiny white ball into holes.

Sport loves hyperbole, but Tiger is beyond sport. His father said it would be so. Earl Woods actually said: 'Tiger will do more than any other man in history to change the course of humanity.' That's quite a claim, for a boy who hadn't even won a major tournament at the time. And when the reporter listening to that asked Earl if he really did think that his son would have more of an impact than Gandhi or the Buddha, Earl said yes. 'He is the bridge between East and West. He is the Chosen One.'

And now he's coming here, to this place.

A concierge sits at a white desk, behind a small pair of angel wings sculpted in silver and a sign that says: 'Whatever'. Whatever you want, the W Hotel can make it happen – provided you can pay. We're just off Times Square, the most electric space in the most electric city in the most electric nation on earth, but in here everyone is meant to be calm and cool. The drifting music, the easeful lighting, the scented candles say: 'Slow down, take it easy, relax. Chill.'

But we can't. None of us can.

There are jugs of juice and water, bowls of nuts and balls of melon, but nothing is being touched. Nobody is eating or drinking, nobody is talking above a whisper. We're all too nervous. There's expectation in the air. And awe. And fear.

The kids from the charity are in awe of Tiger; the staff from the hotel and the foundation are too – but maybe the staff are also a bit afraid of losing their jobs, if something goes wrong in the next few moments. The reporters know careers will be made or broken by what happens in this room. And that includes me. I'm nervous, I have to admit. If Tiger will speak to me I'll walk out of here in the spring of 2011 with the first print interview since his fall from grace. A world exclusive. My editor will be thrilled, the skies will clear, the sun will shine and I will be a happier, healthier human being.

If he doesn't – or if he says nothing remotely interesting – I'll get the sack. I'll lose my job and my income. My children will starve, my love life will vanish and I will be as dust. So, everyone is on edge. This is what it was like in the halls of Montezuma, in the corridors of Versailles, in the kitchen at Graceland. Suffocating, because there can be no air until he comes. He's late, of course. We wait. And we wait. And then we don't.

The lift light flashes, and the doors open. Out step the minders, a couple of retired spooks, I think. They scan the space for trouble, eyes flickering over each of us in turn. Next comes the manager, who looks like a man who is wealthy and powerful and wants to keep it that way. And then: Tiger. Walking with the grace of his namesake, that is true. Looking calm as a heartbeat. Dressed all in black from his toes to his throat, save for the bright white Nike tick on his chest. Saying nothing, meeting no eye, making no sound but the swoosh of his trainers on the carpet.

All around me, bubbles of excitement burst from the children – but they don't rush him. Nobody does. We all stay back. The silence Tiger keeps is like a hand pushing us back against the walls. The silence says: 'Stay where you are and make no sudden movements.' Tiger acknowledges none of us, not even the one guy who does dare approach, to clip a mic on a gym-swollen pec. Tiger just stares into space.

I've never seen a person more spectacularly, deliberately disconnected from those around him. The silence is a weapon. No, a force field. A shield.

This close though, I can see his eyes are as baggy as they must have been in those sleepless days when scandal first broke around him, and his carefully constructed image as a clean-cut, all-American family guy hero fell apart. The passive beauty of his face, so striking in his youth, is hung with shadows.

As a man who apparently loved to prowl casinos in search of winnings, he must know that all the odds are in his favour here today. Things have been arranged that way. He could afford to smile, or say hello to these kids, but he doesn't yet. There's work to do with the journalists. The silence is intimidating. Nobody moves.

When a door opens and Tiger turns to enter a makeshift studio in one of the rooms, and the door closes behind him, there's a collective puffing of the cheeks. Whoah. Was that for real? Is this how he lives, all the time? No wonder he looks so lonely.

*   *   *

Tiger Woods didn't choose to be famous. That choice was made for him by his dad, who put a golf club in his hands when he was barely old enough to walk, but who had set his mind on a fame way beyond golf for his son. This was always a story about control, but Tiger was not the one in command.

Earl Woods served as a Green Beret in the jungles of Vietnam, where he came across psychological warfare. He liked to tell a story about how a snake nearly killed him: it was lying across his face as he woke up from sleep, but his life was saved by a Vietnamese soldier, whose name was Tiger. It wasn't really. That was just what Earl called him.

The point is Earl felt he had been saved for a purpose, which became even more clear to him when his son was born in 1975. The child was registered as Eldrick Tont Woods by his mum, who made the first name up and took the second from Thailand, the land of her birth. But Earl called him Tiger and that was that.

Tiger was going to fulfil Earl's sense of destiny and to do that he needed to become the best at something. Earl chose golf. There was no doubt Tiger had a gift for the game, you could see that from the way he swung the club. The arc of the swing was gorgeous to those who knew about such things and it earned Tiger an invitation to appear on television as a golf prodigy, at the age of two.

He trotted onto the studio floor to jaunty music, *Sesame Street* style, with an oversized red cap, knee-length shorts and white bobbysox, hauling a little golf bag. The audience went: 'Ah!' Earl followed in white pants, a burgundy shirt and a gold medallion. The host and the comedian Bob Hope both stood by in Crimplene suits and sideburns, as Tiger hit a tee shot. Those golfers watching gasped at the beauty of that swing. And that's the clip you'll find if you look online. That was the footage that helped prepare the way for the coming of Tiger Woods, as if he were his own junior John the Baptist. But something else happened in front of the cameras that day, which was seldom replayed in the years that followed and rarely spoken of again. Tiger was asked to play a short putt. He missed. He'd done it a thousand times, even at that age, but the lights were hot, the adults must have loomed large. He took the shot again and missed again.

The pressure had got to him. Earl can't have been pleased.

Over the years that followed he drilled his son, over and over again, training him to block out distractions. He'd do everything he could to put the kid off during his swing or his putt: shouting, swearing, kicking the clubs, whatever it took. Army-style discipline was imposed on the little boy. Earl later admitted using 'military interrogation techniques' on his son, which typically would mean destroying Tiger's confidence then building it up again on new terms. A sports-writer who knew them both well said Earl had 'put Tiger through Vietnam on a golf course'.

Earl also put Tiger into the hands of an old mate from the Navy, a psychologist who hypnotised the boy before and during contests and trained him to use self-hypnosis to get into the zone, so successfully that Tiger later said there were times and tournaments when he just went blank: 'I knew I was there, but I don't remember playing the golf shot.'

That didn't matter. It was working. By the time Tiger turned professional in 1996, he was already famous. He held a press conference to announce his change of status after being signed up for $40 million by Nike, saying simply: 'Hello world.' As the records fell, the dollars flowed: a billion of them, making him the most highly paid sports star of all time. The sponsors adored him. Tiger Woods was young, gifted and black, eloquent and beautiful and victorious. He was following in the footsteps of Muhammad Ali (and in some senses, preparing the way for Barack Obama). At the time of his first great victory, winning the Masters in '97, the Rodney King race riots in Los Angeles were still a burning memory. No sport was more conservative than golf, whose private clubs were havens for racism and bigotry. You couldn't get in if you had the wrong skin, the wrong heritage or the wrong class of parents. Then along came Tiger, breaking all records on a golf course where no black man had ever played. The only black face you ever saw at the Masters course in Augusta was sweating under the strain of carrying a white man's bags, and they were only allowed in to do that seven years before he won. Some people hated him, of course. There were death threats. Damn, he hit the ball so far, they even started rebuilding courses around the country, making them longer so it would be harder for him to win. The black basketball star Charles Barkley said: 'What they're doing to Tiger is blatant racism.' But Tiger played it down. He stayed above race rows. Tiger was a quarter African American. He was half Asian, one eighth Native American and one eighth Dutch. His was the face of the future. Within a decade of that first Masters win, scientists would say the perfect face – the one most attractive to most people in most cultures – was now a soft-toned synthesis of races, a symmetrical, flawless combination of the Asian, the African and the European, just like Tiger. Earl Woods may have been way over the top with his boasts, but he was basically right in believing that if Tiger could win at sport then his ethnicity would allow him to have a much wider impact on society. He'd be a hero.

Let's think about that. The philosopher Hegel says a true hero is inhabited by the *Volksgeist*, or the spirit of his people. Tiger claimed the people of the world as his people. Whether he knew it or not, Tiger was playing by the rules laid down for a hero since classical times. The hero must be absolutely clear about his purpose and let nothing turn him away. The hero must sacrifice everything for his cause, and Tiger had been taught to do that very early. He was blessed with a skill that seemed supernatural, and even had a flashing silver blade, of sorts. Or a whole bag of them. In the absence of war, he proved himself against sporting challenges. In the absence of flesh-and-blood monsters, he fought inequality and injustice.

The true hero must be of value to his community, it is said. Tiger was dedicated, courageous and beautiful. Crucially, he also seemed pure in heart. That's always been required of the hero. As he grew from dazzling young challenger to invincible champion, his image grew too. He married the Swedish model Elin Nordegren, they had two children and now he was a family man. The Tiger Woods Foundation became a serious force for good, distributing millions of dollars, offering real help and hope to children who'd previously had none. This surely provided the platform he would need for a life after golf, when he would run for office. Not that there was any sign of his career fading, as he stayed at the top of the rankings for year after year. The world number one was unstoppable, it seemed. But every hero fails.

*   *   *

How did Tiger feel when Earl had a heart attack and died in 2006? Was he lost without his dad, the man who had chosen fame for him and made it happen? Was that why he blew his reputation, his billion-dollar sponsorship deals and his father's dream? What would Earl say about all that, if he was still alive? I want to know these things, but I'm going to have to be very, very careful about what I ask. This is the most tightly controlled interview I've ever done. The questions have all been approved in advance by email, although I'm planning to risk deviating from the agreed list and take a chance on being thrown out. I've got fifteen minutes with Tiger, a dozen or so questions, depending on how monosyllabic or evasive he chooses to be. Half of them have to be related in some way to a computer game with his name on. That's the reason I'm being allowed into the presence. The trouble is my boss doesn't care about the game. He wants to know about Tiger's life – the very thing I am forbidden from mentioning. The magazine has spent a lot of money getting me here. The stakes are high. My head hurts. My palms are sweating, my breathing is shallow.

And Tiger Woods is in the room suddenly, offering a hand now, but not meeting my eye, of course. There's a poor attempt at a smile, plastered over his mouth like a party mask. The television cameras and lights are all off now, but their crews are still there, packing down. Tiger's entourage is with him, maybe half a dozen people, all watching.

'Er, shall we go into a corner?'

We pull two chairs close to each other and sit, each leaning slightly forward so we might almost whisper to each other. I wish we could, because there are an awful lot of other people here. There's someone from the game's US marketing team, someone from the UK office, Tiger's agent of course and someone else whose name and role I don't catch, but who's going to become important in a minute. They're all standing over or near us as we sit, listening in. And every one of them has an arm stretched out towards us, over our heads, as if praying, but with a phone or recorder on the end, recording every word. I feel cornered, controlled, trapped, under this canopy of hands.

'It's just us,' I say, instinctively, trying to sound calm and like the sort of bloke he'd happily chat to about the secrets of his heart. In the next fifteen minutes.

'Good.'

That's all he says. My mouth is dry as I thank Tiger for his time.

'Yeah,' he says.

I ask – because I have to – how the computer game compares with the real Augusta.

'Obviously, ah, it's not the same experience. But it's as close as it can get. What's amazing, as I was saying, is how closely they have captured the texture of the course . . .' And he's off with a lot of wearily recounted words about how incredibly detailed the game is so that you can see the grass swaying in the wind, to an accuracy of six millimetres or something, blah blah blah. I don't care.

I ask him if he actually plays the game.

'I play as myself.'

Oh, now that's a great image: the fallen, battered hero slumped on his couch in sloppy shorts, scratching his crotch, picking at pretzels and sipping a Bud, playing the Masters one more time through his younger-looking avatar, with his younger body. All you have to do, I say, is press the right button and success comes to you. Wouldn't it be nice if life was like that really?

'It would be nice if golf was a little bit more like that, certainly,' he says smoothly, 'but that's what makes it so difficult.'

We both know he's struggling at the moment. Only a week ago he hit a shot in a tournament that was so bad his playing partner on the day said: 'It's pretty tough not to have a giggle.' I want to ask how it feels to have people who once feared you on the course now laugh at you openly, but again, all I can do is move through the approved questions. I'm not allowed to ask how the death of his father affected him and how life would be different if Earl was still alive, but I can ask how much of an inspiration his father continues to be. It's an anaemic question, typical of a sporting interview, but his answer does seem genuine.

'Ah, man, he's always in mind. There's not a day goes by when I don't think about my dad. My dad and I were very, very, very close. I always miss him. Specially at certain moments, say when my children are doing something and I wish he could have seen that. You know just experiences that you would wish any grandparent could see. My mom is still around, she's able to see it. I wish my dad was around to see it too. My dad has always been close to me and some of his life lessons resonate within me still.'

Now that's interesting. His longest answer so far. The popular theory is that Tiger went off the rails because of the death of his dad: without the man who'd controlled his life, he didn't know how to behave – so he started taking risks and doing things that hurt those around him. It's convenient pop psychology, but it doesn't ring true to me. The behaviour had already started. When Tiger Woods took the call that told him his dad had died, he was not at home with the wife and family but in a beach hut with a cocktail waitress. I can't mention that, though. Obviously. We're almost knee to knee in this hotel room, surrounded by his minders, but we are also completely disconnected from reality. This is the first interview he has given since it all fell apart, but I'm not allowed to ask why that happened. So as a reminder, this is how it unfolded. The *National Enquirer* ran a story in November 2009 saying he had been having an affair with a nightclub promoter in New York called Rachel. A few days later, Tiger somehow crashed his Cadillac into a fire hydrant outside a neighbour's house at two in the morning. There were reports of his wife Elin running after the car during an argument and smashing the rear window with a golf club, in anger. Tiger said his wife had actually broken the window to rescue him from the car. He announced he was taking a break from golf for a while, saying: 'I need to focus my attention on being a better husband, father and person.'

Over the next few months, more women either came forward or were named as his lovers. There was Jaimee, a cocktail waitress, Jaime (a different person with one less 'e'), Kalika, Mindy, Cori, Holly, Julie, Theresa, Loredana, Joslyn, Emma, Devon and Raychel, the twenty-one-year-old daughter of a neighbour. Tiger had known her since she was fourteen. That was said to be the one that caused his wife to fly into a rage.

In February 2010, Tiger made an apology in front of television cameras and an invited audience of friends and family members in Florida, saying: 'I was unfaithful. I had affairs. I cheated. What I did is not acceptable, and I am the only person to blame.' Tiger said he'd come to believe normal rules didn't apply to him, but then he had been trained that way. He didn't say that last bit, actually: I did. What he said was that now he realised it was wrong to see himself as an exception. He was sorry for the hurt he'd caused.

The damage was done, though, to the women and commercially. When Tiger returned to compete in the Masters at Augusta that April, coming fourth, the chairman of the event told the press: 'Our hero did not live up to the expectations of the role model we saw for our children.' The hero must be morally pure, or else he will lose his power. That is the way it has always been, since the beginning of the story. This champion of justice and equality had been caught treating women in a sleazy and exploitative way. He'd departed from his role and broken the deal. Gillette, TAG Heuer, Accenture all dropped Tiger as sponsors, along with AT&T – and so his earnings were said to have fallen by nearly $1 million a week. Elin and Tiger Woods were divorced in August 2010, and she walked away, reportedly, with $110 million.

So, if Earl was still around, to see all that had happened, what would he say?

I know I'm not allowed to ask that question, but I dare to do so in the moment because he just let his guard down and was briefly so tender about his dad. As soon as I do, the chorus around us, collectively, jumps. Looks are exchanged, but Tiger answers. 'Uh. Keep working hard. Keep believing yourself, keep working hard, stay the course.'

Meditation helps, he says. He has embraced his mother's Buddhism more fully. He does seem extraordinarily still at all times. Is that from the meditation?

'I hope so.'

He may be calm, but I'm not. Nine minutes in and I haven't really got much to write about. Time to step things up: 'Tiger, you recently said winning a major was no longer the most important thing in your life. What did you mean?'

'No!'

That's the voice of one of the minders, interrupting quickly before Tiger can answer.

'We, er . . . Cole? We talked about that question in particular . . .'

He tells me it was removed from the list of pre-approved questions.

'Just move on.'

It's that or close down, it's clear. So yes. Let this game of chess continue, and here's my next move. 'Given the success of the Tiger Woods Foundation, would you ever think of taking that good work further by running for office?' This is a spring-loaded question for someone once regarded as a future American president but who must now know there is no way he could get elected. But Tiger is good. He has seen it coming and has an answer ready: 'Well, I'm going to try and build this thing globally.'

No mention of politics there. He's winning at this interview. The minders look satisfied again. We are thirteen minutes and twenty-six seconds into our fifteen-minute session according to the display on the voice recorder – trust me, I look – and I'm beginning to despair. Just then, though, he says something really interesting, out of nowhere: 'I'm not going to be doing this forever. I'm not going to be playing golf forever, there's no doubt, especially at a competitive level. Maybe playing with friends, family, whatever, but at this level? I'm not going to be doing it forever.'

Sorry, what?

Champions just don't talk like this.

Great athletes cannot afford to contemplate failure.

Tiger Woods has always insisted that he's on his way back, that he can dominate the sport again, and yet here he is, saying no, he's not invincible, he can't go on forever. There's something in his tone, too. Cracked, vulnerable, honest, just for a second, like something in the question about his father opened him up and was just sort of there under the surface and then came out. The truth will out. We've all got things we really want to say, even when we're told we shouldn't, by our minders, our bosses or ourselves. Stuff that sits there, desperate to come up. Like one of those toy submarines you play with in the bath. However much you push it down with your fingers, however long it stays submerged, you let it go and it will always come to the surface in the end. And I think that's what's happening here, just for a fleeting moment. The minders can't interrupt. Tiger's the boss and he started talking about this, so I can ask him: how long does he think he has left?

'I don't know. I don't know what that day is, but when that day comes, I will know.'

How?

'I'll just know.'

So that's what I write, when he's shaken my hand and left the room. 'Tiger Woods: I Know I Can't Go On Forever'. It's obvious, in a way, but it also seems horribly like a prophecy in the weeks and months and years that follow, as he falls further and further down the rankings and fails to make the cut in tournaments. Tiger Woods is now a long way from being Gandhi or the Buddha; or even Lee Westwood, who was buying instant mash in a supermarket in Worksop when he took the call to say he was the new number one.

Tiger's swing, his beautiful swing, is destroyed by a bad back. Doctors fuse together the most painful vertebrae in his spine, which most people think means the end of his hopes of returning to the top level of his game. The painkillers become addictive. He's found unconscious behind the wheel of his car on the Florida highway, stationary in a lane of traffic with other vehicles swerving to miss him. His police mugshot shows him looking weary, haggard, broken. He hasn't won a major tournament since we spoke and almost everyone says he never will now. The day he knew was coming has come. Tiger Woods is finished.

*   *   *

Then something truly extraordinary happens, even by the standards of sport, which, as I say, loves hyperbole. Eight years after our interview, two years after hitting rock bottom on the Florida highway, Tiger returns to the Masters at Augusta and becomes a contender again. He is wearing the same kind of bright red shirt and black baseball cap as he used to and from a distance he looks like his younger self.

Like the avatar in the computer game, actually. The walk has changed, though. So has the swing and the face, close up.

Against all the odds he's still in touch with the leaders on the final day. One by one, they drop shots and start to blow their chances. Tiger doesn't look nervous at all. His face is as blank and impassive as it was when he walked down that corridor in the W Hotel. Silence – or at least self-possession – is his shield again, in the middle of the deafening roar of the crowd at the eighteenth hole. Nothing and nobody can touch him, he's making sure of that. He shouldn't be here. He shouldn't be winning. This shouldn't be happening. It doesn't make any kind of sense, except to dreamers. Tiger Woods wins the Masters by a single shot. And then he cracks, grinning and looking bewildered. The cap comes off to reveal a sweaty, whitened, balding forehead and suddenly he's not young Tiger Woods any more. It's a shock to see the true age of the man in his forties who has achieved the completely impossible and matched his younger self.

When Tiger Woods won here for the first time in 1997, he was hugged by his father. This time, the middle-aged man defying time bends down to pick up and hug his own son Charlie, aged nine. His daughter Sam and his mother Tilda are there too. Somebody mentions Earl and Tiger says: 'Life goes on, but there's been one continuity through it all: my mom was there.' Look at her face, if you can find a clip online. He's still her little boy, this big, weary champion. More so than ever, without Earl dominating. Very few people have ever really known what was going on inside the head of Tiger Woods, just like we don't know why he treated those women so very badly. There's no excuse for that, no excuse for all the hurt he caused. And there is no real redemption to be gained from hitting a ball into a succession of holes with a stick, whatever stories we tell about it for entertainment.

But I remember something he said in the W Hotel: 'I am trying to become a better person. I am trying to become a better person with my kids. A better father.' That was the aspiration he repeated, through the confessions and the attempted comebacks.

When we met, he seemed utterly disconnected, isolated, alone, lost, like a man trying to find his way back home. As I watch Tiger Woods, after his astonishing win at the Masters, hug his daughter, his son and his mum, I can only hope he's found it.

*   *   *

Nelson

The editor called: 'Get on a plane. Mandela's dying.'

'Okay, when?'

'Now. He's dying now. Get on a plane!'

Okay. Right. Drop everything then, just like that? Friends, family, appointments, medical stuff, birthdays? Sure. 'How long am I going for, boss?'

'I don't know. How long will it take him to die? Then there's the funeral. This is the big one. A month?'

I was sent upstairs to a health and safety expert, who frowned.

'Things are volatile right now. There could be a revolution in South Africa. You'll need a week's hostile environment training. We'll give you all the right kit, but it takes a while to organise. When are you leaving?'

'Er, tonight.'

'Oh dear.'

I left his office with some advice on where to keep my money, how not to be followed and who to ring in the event of a violent insurrection.

'We'll try and get you out,' he said breezily. 'Good luck!'

So I dashed home to kiss the kids before going to Heathrow to catch a plane heading south in the summer of 2013, feeling sick. I'd been to other parts of Africa before, but only in the worst of circumstances. Working for a relief charity, meeting the sick and the desperately poor. I'd been scared and miserable then and I didn't massively want to go back, but it wasn't like there was a choice. Nelson Mandela was a giant of the twentieth century. His passing would be a world event. As an icon he was up there with Elvis and Marilyn. Okay, maybe Gandhi is more appropriate. This was an honour though, to be trusted to write about an historic moment. The first draft of history, they call journalism. Sometimes that's right. And sometimes the first draft comes bloody quickly. 'I want two thousand words on the situation by Saturday morning,' said the editor, fully aware that my plane would not touch down in Jo'burg until the Friday night. I'd have no time to talk to anyone or get any sense of what was going on, but they wanted to be able to show the readers I was there. 'We'll get you the cuts,' he said breezily and a series of cuttings duly appeared in my emails, to read on the plane. Sometimes, it seems, the secret to being a foreign correspondent is that you've seen the local media and your reader hasn't. I also had the *Rough Guide to Nelson Mandela*, a copy of his autobiography, a long flight and eyes that wouldn't stay open, but when I landed, the adrenaline kicked in.

I went straight to the Mediclinic Heart Hospital in Pretoria, where Mandela was said to be on kidney dialysis and – as a member of the family put it – using machines to breathe. People were milling about in the half-light outside the hospital. Hundreds of them, without any purpose other than to be there. To be close, somehow. They called him by his tribal name: Madiba. Or Tata, a word for father. And he was not dead yet. One hand-written note pinned to the fence said: 'If you can beat prison, you can beat this.'

Sadly, that felt unlikely.

*　　*　　*

The man had spent twenty-seven years in prison for his resistance to apartheid, some of it in solitary confinement, some out in the blinding sun breaking rocks, some talking with his guards, becoming friends with them, formulating ideas about forgiveness that would help South Africa heal. Someone had put up giant screens in the street showing scenes from his life: from the black and white footage of his trial in the sixties to the day in 1990 he took a long walk to freedom, from prison to the outside world. The images played silently. Few people spoke. They watched the face of Mandela change from a young man to a rebel to a prisoner, then a president. I looked over their heads to the square, concrete hospital, wondering if he was in any of those rooms, behind any of those window blinds. Trying to think of him there, this frail ninety-four-year-old, lying in a bed surrounded by tubes, with his third wife Graça in an armchair by his side maybe, holding his hand. I was thinking of the click of the ventilator, the mechanical breath, the blip of the monitors and the heavier, laboured breathing of those who were allowed near and who felt themselves about to lose him.

*　　*　　*

What is it that makes people stand outside a hospital at a time like that, with no way of reaching the person they are thinking of, talking about, singing about, praying for?

The desire to connect, perhaps. Or to give thanks.

A young black man in a peaked cap and the blue uniform of the police stepped past me through the crowd, with formal precision. We all moved aside, instinctively. The police officer placed a lighted candle on the floor, straightened up, held himself taller and saluted a portrait of Mandela that had been pinned to the hospital gates. Then he took off his cap and bowed his head. Now I noticed there were others like him all around me, a dozen or so of them, singing along with the slow, mournful song of the crowd, clapping in time,

35

swaying with an easy elegance. 'Don't cry, little one, God is watching.'

Those were the words of the song, in the Tsonga language. It seemed a gentle thing, a lullaby. The first policeman stepped back and his shoulders dropped as he rejoined his friends. Another took his place to salute the portrait; then another and another in turn. Behind them was a man I took to be their leader, because of the set of his face and the heft of his body and not just because he was the only white policeman there. He was cupping a candle with two big hands, the light playing on a bushy ginger moustache.

When the ceremony was over, I approached and saw tears in his eyes. 'Colonel Karl,' he said, a little reluctantly. But when I asked what he was doing there he answered without hesitation: 'Madiba is such a treasure to us.' I was surprised to hear the tribal name spoken with such tenderness by an Afrikaner, but then I'd only just arrived in the country and didn't yet realise how people felt. 'He will go down in history as one man who showed the world the second commandment of the Lord: that we must love each other.'

The colonel had grown up among white farmers. The Sharpeville massacre had taken place when he was three years old, but it was a long way from his home. 'As a child you didn't understand. My best friends were young African guys. We were playing together, I could learn to speak Sotho a little from them and when we were naughty my father was giving us all together a hiding. He left me until last to give me the best hiding. I ate with them and learned their traditions. It was not strange to me. That is, I believe, how come I am still around here today.'

Apartheid was in full force back then, though. 'All whites were forced to serve in the army for at least two years. You didn't have a choice.' He was able to serve in the police instead. 'I had provincial colours as a junior in athletics. The police were eager for sporty young lads, to bolster their image.' That was in 1975, the year before 600 protesters were shot and killed during the Soweto uprising. I wondered how he felt about the way his own police force behaved under apartheid?

'There have been significant changes over the years,' said the colonel, carefully. 'It is unfortunate what happened under previous national commissions of the police. I will never say anything bad about them. It is not for me to make a judgement about that. I was not there. I did not investigate anything.'

He did, however, work for the last two presidents of the apartheid era. This man had been a member of the security team for F. W. de Klerk. And he had seen for himself the rising pressure for change, coming from far beyond South Africa. 'I can still remember the huge batch of post that would arrive there every day. There were people appointed to open that post, to screen it for parcel bombs and other threats. As I recall, three quarters or more was from all over the globe, saying "Release Mandela." There was an outcry. We could see that and were saying to each other: "This man Mandela is a very special person."'

Mandela was already world famous. In England we boycotted South African apples and danced to a song by The Special AKA calling for his release – and my boss on the local paper in the East End of London, who liked to play tricks on young reporters, sent a very young intern down to the butcher's shop for an interview about their special offer.

'Ask them about it,' he said, hiding his smirk. 'They're doing it all week.'

So the workie, who was not much more than a kid, asked for his Free Nelson Mandela. The butcher answered with two words, one of which I can't repeat.

When Mandela was eventually released in 1990, some Afrikaners prepared for war. They had been raised to see the likes of him as the enemy. 'Wherever you would go at that time, at parties or family gatherings, people were talking about what was going to happen if the ANC won the election in 1994,' said the colonel. 'The fear was there. People were collecting lots of tins of food and extra ammunition for firearms. Only the whites could possess firearms legally. However, the weapons of mass destruction were with the army and so on. What would happen if these were to be in the hands of the former enemy?'

He was choosing his words carefully. 'That is what lots of people were fearing. There would be a civil war and they would be defenceless.' That didn't happen. The colonel had come to the hospital gates all these years later out of love and gratitude. 'There was fear among the white people but Madiba changed their minds with his personality. He was also like a father figure to people in the ANC and they listened to him.'

A young black female constable said: 'I'm here today because of Madiba. I never thought I'd share an office with a white man.'

Now, though, people were worried. Fearful. Without Mandela – without that calming presence and reminder of the recent, inspirational past – would there be violence? The colonel knew that if there was, his officers would be in the thick of it. 'We know he must go at sometime. All of us must go. But we pray Madiba will be able to continue his mission with us for a little longer, because there is so much still to be done.'

*   *   *

The rest of the world was talking about Mandela the legend, but people in South Africa talked about him as a man. An ordinary man, with failings. Not a great husband to his first wife Evelyn, not a great father to his own children, before prison and after. At the Mandela museum in Soweto, where you could walk through his old living room from the sixties, I looked down at the big brown armchair and thought about all the nights he wasn't there. Out fighting the fight, keeping up the struggle, seeing other women. That was part of the Nelson Mandela story too. An elderly gentleman called Joseph told me: 'I was a young man when he was a young man, we behaved as young men do. When you think that he became the father of our nation, a hero to the world . . . well, it is a very big miracle. Madiba made you believe in miracles.' They happened around him, that was the point. They happened through him, but also in spite of his failings. 'We know Madiba,' said Joseph. 'We know him as a man.'

I learned that Nelson and Evelyn were married for fourteen years. They had four children. A daughter died when she was just nine months old. Evelyn found consolation in religion.

Nelson got deeper and deeper into politics. Then later a son was killed in a car crash at the age of twenty-four. Another son was lost to an AIDS-related illness when he was fifty-five. So never mind the struggle, as a father there were deep sorrows.

Only their daughter Makaziwe survived – and as he lay in hospital now, she was fighting a legal battle for control of the Mandela trusts. Evelyn was dead, but her offspring were known as the First Family. She'd always kept out of the spotlight. Nelson Mandela's second wife Winnie had not. She was a political firebrand, forceful and eloquent. They were married for nearly four decades, including all the years in prison during which time Winnie built up a power base of her own. She was accused of human rights abuses but survived as a leading member of the ANC. Winnie and her daughters were known as the Second Family. Her grand-daughters were starring in a thirteen-part reality series called *Being Mandela*, revealing lives full of bling. You had to wonder what Grandpa made of that.

Winnie gave press conferences at the gates of the hospital describing herself as 'the senior member of this family' and talking about Nelson as 'our husband'. They'd been divorced for years. The woman by his bedside was Graça Machel, the widow of the former president of Mozambique, who had married Mandela on his eightieth birthday. Desmond Tutu said Graça brought Nelson happiness in old age and he called her 'a strong woman of enormous stature. Gracious, but not to be trifled with or underestimated.'

So those were the wives and children, but now many of Mandela's seventeen grandchildren and fourteen great-grandchildren seemed to have a sense of ownership of this ailing man and his lucrative name, particularly Mandla, the eldest grandson and the patriarch. He'd dug up the bodies of Mandela's three lost children from their graves in the family ancestral village of Qunu in the Eastern Cape. Mandla moved them to his own village, thirteen miles away, where he'd built a visitor centre and he seemed to believe Grandad would agree to be buried there instead. Great for tourism. But other members of the Mandela family had just taken Mandla to court, while the old man was lying there dying, and they won the right for the bodies to be dug up again and put back.

Tribal leaders said they were upsetting the ancestors with all this.

Tutu pleaded with the family: 'Please, please, please may

we think not only of ourselves? It is almost like spitting in Madiba's face.'

*   *   *

He didn't die. He left the hospital. I came home, after three weeks of waiting outside. Then five months later, just before midnight at the start of December 2013, came the call.

'Get on a plane, Mandela's dying.'

What? Again?

I didn't say that, of course. I got back on a plane two hours later, and while I was in the air the death was announced. South Africa was suddenly released into mourning. The whole world joined in. The British and American media started Mandelamania.

Barack Obama flew in to be the star turn of a chaotic memorial event at a football stadium, where the heavens opened and the stands emptied. It was miserable. The thing most people remember is that a sign language interpreter on stage with the American president was exposed as, well, making it all up. Whatever he thought he was saying with those hand gestures didn't have much to do with the speech. The poor man was ridiculed. Afterwards, he claimed to have suffered a schizophrenic episode and seen angels.

'Madiba is dead. We are grateful for having had him among us, now we must live,' said a man outside selling T-shirts and caps bearing the name.

The traders needed to sell the icon in order to eat. The Mandela family was doing everything it could to capitalise. The politicians were wrapping themselves up in his mantle as a useful disguise, including the big ones.

'It took a man like Mandela to liberate not just the prisoner but the jailer as well,' said Barack Obama, positioning himself as the heir to all that.

The global icon of Mandela was growing fast after his death, getting further and further from reality, until all there would be left of him was the smile.

I watched an American reporter talking to camera about how South Africans worshipped Mandela, but in truth it was people outside the country who worshipped him. South Africans were much more pragmatic. The ones I met talked about his flaws: the emotional distance, the poor decisions as a president, the dubious deals, the questionable choice of successor, to name a few. A street preacher with fire in her eyes started telling me about King David, a hero of two faiths, who was a deeply flawed man: 'God used him anyway!' Still, almost everyone I spoke to felt a powerful gratitude for real, gritty reasons.

'I had to come and sleep over so I can be closer. I want to say thank you,' said a nurse called Mashuda as she waited in the street to see the ambulance carrying the coffin come past. She held a yellow rose. 'The changes he brought into my life are so many. I'm a professional nurse because of Madiba. If it was not for him I would still be working as an assistant, with no prospects.'

When the black Mercedes undertaker ambulance came by, with windows showing the coffin wrapped in the national flag, she threw her rose. I'd seen this before in England after the death of Diana, Princess of Wales. There was gratitude for sure, but the people who stood on the streets for Madiba seemed to be like moths drawn to a light, like weary travellers drawn to a warming flame. Good things had happened around him. He carried that in his presence, even now. They wanted to be near it. I thought about a Sam Cooke song and the story of the lady who reached out for her Lord, thinking that if she could just touch the hem of his garment she would be made whole.

Mashuda couldn't touch the body of her fallen hero, or even one of his fancy shirts, but she could send a flower spiralling through the air and see it bounce off the bonnet of the big black van in which he lay. That was contact. That was something.

*　　*　　*

The personal, intimate thing – for those who could make it – was to see Nelson Mandela lying in state. Face to face with the president, although not much of a chance to chat.

I was thrilled to be sent. I wanted to be close to this man, even if it had to be after death. So did Bono, apparently. Naomi Campbell too. They didn't have to queue.

A pensioner from Pennsylvania called Sharon said she'd travelled for two days to be there. 'I have regretted for fifty years not going to see John F. Kennedy after he was shot. I don't have another fifty years to regret not coming here.'

Most people were not icon collectors. The line snaked for miles through Pretoria's grid of streets and up to the Union Buildings, the seat of the South African government. The wait was long. Umbrellas were held as shelter from the sun. We shuffled forward in single file and some sang or hummed. The songs of freedom. Parents bent down and told their hot and bothered children why this man mattered. But on the last few sandstone steps to where Madiba lay, each of us fell silent in turn. He lay under a large arch, like a stage set, outdoors. This place had been built to show off the power of the Boers, but President Nelson Mandela had chosen not to tear down the statues or close the Union Buildings. He had chosen to occupy the space. He was still doing that now.

A pair of marines in dazzling white uniforms stood guard with their heads bowed. The coffin was draped in white silk, with glass over the open part.

And there he was, suddenly. Nelson Mandela himself, dressed in a dark shirt with swirls.

Lying on his back. Eyes closed, head tilted a little.

This was him.

Close enough you could reach out and touch him, although you'd get into a lot of trouble if you did. It didn't look like him, though. Not like the face on all the posters. He was pale, bloated. Harassed, not serene. Not an icon of peace.

There was no time to stare, just a second or two with the body before an usher gave a signal to move on, back into the open from under the canopy and down the steps on wobbly legs, carried forward by the momentum of the line.

I sat down in the garden, where the air was heavy with the thick scent of many flowers. I had to sit down. Trembling, ambushed by feelings I couldn't process. There was an overwhelming sense of absence. The body I'd just seen was a husk. A snakeskin, discarded. His light and his energy were elsewhere. He had moved on. If the man's soul had been oceanic, as everybody said it was, using a word to describe how it stretched around the world touching every shore, the body was a piece of washed-up driftwood.

'He's not here,' said a woman in her Sunday best, coming down the steps, face wet with tears. 'He's not here.'

He was everywhere, instead. The man had gone away, leaving only his body. The lover, the father, the friend, gone. But his face was everywhere. His memory was everywhere. His effect was everywhere. Living in the people, or at least in their hopes.

As Tutu says: 'I am, because we are.'

If you can find a way of connecting with people as Mandela did, if you can believe we are interdependent, good and bad; if you can make people feel better about themselves, help them to forgive, to let go of the anger and hurt that hurts them, and find release, and live together side by side, even in disagreement, even as flawed, broken human beings; if you can do that yourself – forgive and be forgiven – if you can believe there is something more to aim for, something higher, and help others get there too, then maybe you can, like Mandela, become bigger than yourself.

*   *   *

I went to the funeral, at the village of Qunu in the Eastern Cape. Well, I was allowed to park up with the rest of the reporters on a ridge overlooking the valley, a patchwork of green and brown fields separated by chicken-wire fences and dotted with circular huts and two-room shacks. The one exception was the house of the Mandelas, surrounded by trees, with a sloping red-tiled roof. It looked like an out-of-town Tesco. Next to this were a couple of vast white marquees, for the guests including presidents and kings, Prince Charles and Oprah Winfrey. And beyond that, a small white canopy over the grave itself. Security was very tight. One of us reporters paid a villager for the chance to lie among the goats in an outhouse way down below, within the ring of steel; but after a sleepless night on the mud floor with the animals they'd been found out and marched back up the hill by soldiers.

Little boys from the outskirts of the village ran about among us with excitement, as six propeller-driven aircraft with South African flags on their tails flew very low over the valley, followed by the boom of five fighter jets. The boys cried out: 'Qunu! Qunu!'

Then there was silence on the hillside.

One of the boys was sitting on the bonnet of my car, and he told me what I hoped was his name: 'Lukanu.'

'Cole,' I said, fist at my heart. He smiled and nodded, and pointed to the pair of binoculars hanging at my chest. I said: 'Do you want a go?'

He was about ten or eleven. Same age as my kids back home.

I got the impression he'd never looked through a pair of these before, so I watched his face as he held them up to his eyes, squinted and tried to see through, struggled to fix them on the right place; then, from his expression, I guess he saw it: the white canopy over the grave itself, far away across the valley but now, close up, as the lenses defied the rules and showed what was possible. Now he was there, in his mind, sitting among the VIPs as the music played. A very special person. Suddenly, for a moment, the world looked different, looked how it could be: the barriers had dropped and he was included.

I'll never forget that smile.

*　　*　　*

Desmond

The end of the world was coming, apparently. There were Messiahs everywhere. A young man from Colorado was arrested for provoking bloodshed after saying he would be killed on the streets of the city then rise again on the third day. The blood shed would have been his own, but they deported him anyway.

A student was found wandering the desert half naked, calling himself John the Baptist, although it wasn't clear who was meant to be his Christ. There were plenty of candidates. Messiah fever, they called it. Every few days, someone else would declare themselves the Second Coming, out there on the streets of Jerusalem, a city where Christians were only competing to be heard alongside Muslims and Jews.

This is a story about Desmond Tutu, the great South African campaigner, but it starts in Jerusalem in 1999. It was chaos. Glorious chaos. Full of beauty and danger. And this thrilling, clashing city was fully open to visitors, for the moment. There was peace, of a kind, and tourists could come with a freedom that would soon be gone.

I was there to do a piece on pilgrimage for the *Independent* with a bunch of people from the Church in Wales, pilgrims of a kind I felt friendly towards, even if I didn't share their faith any more. I knew their stories and the sacred texts, but I had lost my faith, during a difficult part of my life a couple of years before and wasn't quite sure where I stood on it all. I was there as an observer, allegedly detached, but actually wondering how to react to this place where faith mattered;

where faith had been a matter of life and death for so long. Was it all just bonkers? Or was there something beyond all the tourism and strife that I could still connect with, even in my unbelief?

*   *   *

The streets were rammed with people around the gleaming golden Dome of the Rock, the third holy place of Islam after Mecca and Medina. I found myself almost standing cheek to cheek for a moment with a young woman in a black hijab, her features sharpened by fasting during Ramadan and her eyes alive with awe at this place. An elderly lady in white, perhaps her grandmother, was making rapid movements with her hands as she mumbled prayers, eyes half closed. The official hour of prayer was approaching, and soon all non-believers would be asked to leave; but for the moment, we shuffled behind each other, in single file, shoeless and mild. For once, the tour parties were quiet and respectful, overpowered by the intensity of the atmosphere. The flat white rock behind a wooden balustrade had been sacred for so long and to so many: it was said to be the place where Abraham brought his son to be sacrificed; where the Holy of Holies stood in Solomon's temple; where the curtain was torn in two on the day of crucifixion; and where Muhammad ascended to heaven.

Outside, under a cloudless sky, we walked down to the ancient limestone of the Western Wall. The most holy place in Judaism, the last remaining fragment of the temple. Men in black hats, long black coats and matching beards rocked and beat time with their feet as they recited the Psalms. Younger men in prayer shawls passed scrolls around, while their women watched and took photos from outside the enclosure. A teenager with a phylactery tied to his forehead wore Israeli army combat gear. His tallit shawl only half covered an automatic rifle.

Beyond, over the rooftops of the walled city, was the Church of the Holy Sepulchre, revered as the site of Christ's death, burial and resurrection. Just before dawn I'd watched a Coptic priest in a black skullcap stand in that echoing church, chanting his liturgy to nobody but God. Now the sun was high the place would be tight with tourists and their guides. And something did strike me, standing there at the Western Wall. An epiphany, if you like. A revelation, although perhaps an ordinary one.

Something had been going on here in this part of Jerusalem for a long time.

In this corner of one of the many cities on earth, the central events – the central stories, anyway – of three major religions had all, allegedly, taken place.

Just here.

Abraham standing over his son, trying to work out why the God who had told him to kill the boy was now saying no. The rip in the temple fabric – the tear in the history of humanity – as Jesus hung on the cross. The beat of the wings of the horse-like beast called Buraq as it bore the Prophet up to heaven. Those were some of the tales told of the things that happened here. There were many others. But what were they, really? A conversation of sorts, in this place. A strange, fractured dialogue between humans and the divine.

I didn't understand it. I couldn't shake off how maddening, frustrating and heart-breaking some of it had been – and still was. All that hurt. But I was suddenly able to see it as a bunch of broken people trying to make sense of glimpses they had seen of something more. And I knew in my bones I couldn't walk away. Not entirely.

Thankfully, none of those I toured the holy sites with believed they were the Son of God. 'Some of the details may be mythical,' said one of the bishops. 'That doesn't bother me.' Nor did they believe the Four Horsemen of the Apocalypse were about to bring morning coffee, although we did visit the plain of Megiddo, which is where the Bible says Armageddon will begin. And this was 1999; we were on the verge of a flip of the calendar that some saw as ushering in the End Times. The visitor centre in Megiddo had a webcam trained on the plain, so I wrote a news story saying 'The End of the World Will Be Televised'. Just for a bit of fun. There was so much reaction to the piece online they took the webcam down, so a week later I wrote another story: 'The End of the World Will Not Be Televised'. That was the headline I'd really wanted, because of the Gil Scott-Heron song 'The Revolution Will Not Be Televised', which is about something else altogether. These are the games we journalists sometimes play with ourselves, as a defence mechanism against the huge, terrifying ideas we are dealing with. And it doesn't get much more terrifying than Armageddon, does it? I believed in it once, completely. Now, not so much, although the idea of the Y2K bug causing computers to malfunction on New Year's Eve and planes to drop out of the sky was distinctly worrying. And I was maybe a bit nostalgic for my days of certainty, when I'd known what the hell was happening in the world and how to deal with it. So even though I was profoundly disenchanted with religion and religiosity, and had lost my old faith, I was looking for a way to connect with whatever might be behind and beyond all that. And something did happen in Jerusalem that was completely unexpected and surprising, like being mugged by God. It was emotional, but rooted in the natural.

We were at the Pool of Bethesda, the place in the city where the sick and ailing would come in search of healing in the old times. Once a day, the legend said, an angel would stir the waters and whoever was in them or touched by them could be blessed. I've heard that the stirring of the waters actually came from the temple altar being cleaned, the blood of the sacrificial lamb being washed away and the mixture of blood and water going down into the drainage system, eventually reaching the pool and causing ripples, which were taken to be the actions of an angel. I don't know if that's true, but blood and sacrifice and cleansing, that's a very old idea. One of the oldest. Again, I was struggling though. These were just ruins. Crowded, faded remains. None of it meant anything, until I found myself going down some steps to stand beside a pool of dark water.

Nobody else was there.

Suddenly it was me and the water and the stones that made the high walls around me and the blue sky up above.

Nothing else.

Suddenly it was elemental.

Suddenly I could feel connected, somehow, like I was there, back then, when things happened. This was all instinctive, not thought out. I was just reacting. Feeling.

And as I did, I became aware of someone coming down to stand behind me. One of the Welsh group I was with. I didn't know his name then, or I'd forgotten it. He knelt down beside me, wordlessly, and scooped up water from the pool. Then he stood with it still cupped in his hands and turned to me. And he looked me in the eyes, still without saying anything.

My hands happened to be clasped together. He poured the water over them and enclosed my hands with his. I felt the cold water, then the warmth of his skin.

He was looking at me with kindness. Then he smiled. He nodded. He dropped his hands and walked away, back up the steps, leaving me there, and I wept.

I still don't know why.

*   *   *

The Welsh were on what they called a Living Stones pilgrimage. They would go to see the Holy Land and all the usual sites, but they would also visit fellow believers in Jerusalem, the West Bank and Gaza. Life has not been easy for Christians in those places. It's not been easy for anyone. So it was that we took a coach out of the city to a place two hours north, where the Bishop of Jerusalem was to celebrate communion and we were to meet Palestinians. There were not many of us – from memory only thirty or so – who gathered in a chapel to take the bread and wine that are for some the body and blood of Christ.

I was there as an observer. That's what I told myself again. Then the bishop announced that he had a friend coming to speak to us and in walked a man whom some considered a living saint and I certainly saw as a hero: Desmond Tutu, Archbishop of Cape Town, hero of the struggle against apartheid, leader of the attempt to bring truth, reconciliation and therefore healing to his country, against all the odds. Friend and ally of Nelson Mandela. Winner of the Nobel Prize for Peace. Blimey. The congregation received him with a joy that might only have been matched by the Second Coming.

Tutu was approaching seventy at this point, he looked more tired and older and smaller than when I had seen him on the television, but we later learned he was on a private visit to meet members of the Israeli government and Yasser Arafat, the President of the Palestinian National Authority.

That must have been a bit stressful. The old peacemaker was trying to work his magic here. And when he spoke, it was electrifying.

Even in weariness, his voice had an intensity that lifted us, an authority that came from experience and a clarity that was thrilling.

He drew a clear parallel between the suffering of black people in South Africa under apartheid and that of the Palestinians. I wrote down what he said: 'I told my people, "These others might think that you are nothing. They may trample on your dignity with hobnail boots but know that God loves you with a love that will not let you go." ' Then he turned to the bishop and said: 'Our God. Your God. The same yesterday, today, forever.'

If change could come to South Africa, he was saying, it could come anywhere, including here. I could almost believe it, in that moment. Being with him felt special. Was that because he was a wonderful human being? I wasn't sure.

He was energetic, and he had an entertaining way of chuckling, a persuasive way of jabbing the air while he was making a point, frowning for the difficult bits and breaking into a wide, winning smile. But I also had the feeling this elfin man was really quite human – and I was about to find out how true that was.

Afterwards, there was a lunch with extraordinarily good food and stories that warmed and broke the heart, as well as some lengthy and stupefying speeches. A twelve-year-old girl sang a song about the lives lost during the uprising called the Intifada. I was sitting there the whole time frantically trying to remember what I knew about Tutu and what on earth I could ask him, because somehow I had managed to persuade his people that it would be okay, even a good idea, if he let me interview him. 'Sure,' they said. 'After the lunch. We're driving back to Jerusalem. Come with us, sit in the back and talk to him.'

This was astonishing. A career-defining moment for a kid who had not been on the nationals long. The chance to get a story out of a man who had been at the centre of one of the biggest stories of our time in South Africa and who was now apparently at the centre of another, even bigger story: the Middle East peace process.

More than that, on a personal level, I was about to be close up with a man I really admired. I spent half the time trying to think of sensible questions and half the time panicking that I was not up to this. Not by a long shot. Then the time came. The speeches ended. Goodbyes were said. Tutu and his people moved towards their vehicles. Again, from memory I think he was in a black diplomatic car, of the kind you find at embassies, presumably with bulletproof windows.

The minders were in suits, with sunglasses hiding anxious eyes.

They knew what was happening though.

They knew it was okay for me to be there.

They knew it was all right if I opened the door of the car.

They watched me get in.

I got in.

And he screamed.

He yelped, maybe.

I know it was primal. I know there was panic and fear in it.

I know it was a shock to find him yelling at me: 'Get out! Get out of my car!'

The Nobel Peace Prize winner shouting in my face.

And with good reason. Nobody had told him.

He didn't know who I was. He didn't know what I wanted.

He only saw this big blond stranger get in next to him, in this troubled foreign land. He must have thought he was about to die. I would have screamed too.

I got out fast; one of the minders who was still standing there shrugged and his car left in a hurry, without me.

Gone.

Absolutely gone.

I stood there watching the dust cloud settle again, feeling a bit stupid. Wondering what had just happened, with the connection I was longing for, the moment of humanity between us, broken in tiny pieces on the floor.

*   *   *

The next time I saw him was in South Africa in December 2013, so fourteen years later. The country was mourning the death of Mandela, and I was there to report. Giddy and confused and still adjusting, trying to find something to say about this great moment of national and international convulsion and sorrow but also celebration, I found myself that Sunday at another Mass, this time to celebrate Mandela's life, in Soweto at the Catholic church of Regina Mundi, Queen of the World.

Some of the thousand or so people there wore ANC scarves, others their own colours. The Sodality of the Immaculate Heart came in their powder-blue uniforms, looking like holy nurses. They danced to songs and hymns in English, Zulu and Xhosa and it was strange to be standing among them with other members of the media, wishing I could dance too. Watching the photographers move among the mourners, cool and dispassionate at first, thinking of nothing but getting the shot, even if it meant blocking an aisle, being in the way, focused and intent, but then slowly being won over, because the music and the dancing and the smiles, and the tears, and the warmth, were contagious. By the end, their body language had changed. They were smiling, their cameras down, letting the moment and the emotion touch them. They'd got the shot but they'd also got the point.

Here, there were still bullet holes in the ceiling. This was the spiritual heart of the biggest township in the old days, a centre for the struggle against apartheid, the place to which young people fled for sanctuary during the Soweto uprising of 1976, when the police entered and opened fire. A church described by Mandela when he came back as president after twenty-seven years in prison as 'a battlefield between the forces of democracy and those who did not hesitate to violate a place of religion with tear gas, dogs and guns'.

It was also a place where Desmond Tutu had come with the Truth and Reconciliation Commission to hear those who wanted to be heard. Tutu heard hundreds of testimonies from people who had been beaten, tortured, imprisoned or bereaved, and from people who had done those things, who wanted to own up to them and tell the truth in the hope that it might set them free, at least emotionally. Or that they would be given amnesty for saying so. Families were finally able to confront those who had hurt or killed their loved ones. Hidden bodies were discovered and given decent burials. Secret crimes were brought into the open. The history of apartheid and all its sins was laid bare.

Some people saw this as truth without justice, but South Africa did begin to heal a little. Tutu played his part. And at the root of it was a thing he called 'ubuntu', which he expressed in five words: 'I am, because we are.'

This was his take on a way of living and being he said he'd learned from tribal and traditional beliefs: that we are only able to be fully human when we are with other humans. He called it: 'The ancient spirituality of humanity's oneness with our creator, the other and nature. We are all one.'

If that sounds a bit high-minded, there's no point in me trying to sum it up. Let me quote him: 'Ubuntu is the essence of being human and it says a solitary human being is a contradiction in terms. I can't be a human being on my lonesome. I wouldn't know how to speak as a human being. I wouldn't know how to think as a human being. I wouldn't know how to walk as a human being. I have to learn from other human beings how to be human – and so ubuntu says my humanity is bound up in yours. I am, only because you are. We then say a person is a person through other persons, and that we need this communal harmony if we are going to survive at all.'

The survival of the species has always depended on human beings working together for mutual protection and support, said Tutu, who had witnessed or been told about many terrible deeds but never stopped believing that people are essentially good. Made for goodness, to quote the title of one of his books. Forgiveness was a way to healing, he said in the television interview I just quoted. 'Anger and revenge and bitterness are corrosive of this harmony. Forgiving is not being altruistic, you're not being nice to the other guy. You're actually being nice to yourself. Forgiving, apart from anything else, is actually good for your health.' He chuckled when he said that, in his infectious way. And there's something else Desmond Tutu said that still makes a huge impact on me: 'God is not a Christian!'

Think about that for a moment. The Archbishop of Cape Town is saying it. He's doing so as an African brought up to believe in the invisible world, the world of the spirit, even before he was a Christian.

'All of us belong to God. God reveals God to all of us and we have different understandings of God,' he said in an interview with Christian Egge of the magazine *Herald of Europe* in 2006. 'I don't believe I have a God who sits and worries that a Buddhist may come up with a wonderful idea. I do not feel obliged to think it cannot be a good idea just because it is a Buddhist idea. No, I am thrilled that a Hindu could be such a leading exponent of non-violence, and affect and influence so many people as Mahatma Gandhi did. I am not upset that one of the most brilliant scientists, Einstein, happens to be a Jew. You see it points to the wonderful bounty of God that none of us has a proprietary claim on God. God is God, God is forever free.'

And that takes me back to the Western Wall, to the Dome of the Rock, to the Pool of Bethesda and the feeling in my gut that something wild and crazy and real and bigger than all our stories, rules and rituals has been happening.

*   *   *

They say rain is a blessing, because it brings life. The day after Regina Mundi there was a downpour. I felt the rain come down hard on my neck and shoulders as I stood at the back of a marquee, half in and half out, waiting to see if there would be room at the tribute to Mandela that was being held at his charity foundation's headquarters in Johannesburg. The Soweto Gospel Choir was to sing. All Madiba's old allies were there. His closest companions on the long walk to freedom. And it felt like a family affair, something close and intimate, on a humid night, under the thundering rain, as Tutu took the microphone and hit that room like lightning. 'What would have happened had Madiba died in prison?'

That made them gasp. They knew the truth.

'Wonderfully, of course, the anti-apartheid movement triumphed and sent that vicious system reeling into the gutters of history.'

Peering through his spectacles, giggling occasionally at his own jokes, rolling his words with relish, baring his teeth in a smile and jabbing that finger in the air again, he talked about his friend's first night of freedom, spent at Tutu's official residence in Cape Town. 'He did something I have seen him do many, many times. When he went to a banquet Madiba would go to the kitchen and thank the staff. Because Madiba was really saying to people: "Not many of us are VIPs but all of us are VSPs."'

We got there before him, of course. Some of us had heard this before.

'Very Special Persons.'

Then he shouted: 'Now I want you to stand, to pay homage to Madiba and say: "I am a VSP!"'

So we did. The cynic in me kicked in, of course. This was monumentally cheesy. On another level though, that night, it was beautiful. These were people who had lived through the hardest of times together and seen terrible things; but who had also seen miracles in their country. They were sad at their loss but grateful too and willing to share their friend with the world. Finally, I felt a sense of connection with him and with everybody else in the room, which I had not earned, but which was being given freely, with such generosity and grace. Not like when he chucked me out of his car, but a bit like the way I felt when that stranger scooped the water from the Pool of Bethesda, held my hands and looked into my eyes. Finally, I could say with Desmond Tutu and all the rest of us lesser mortals in the room: 'I am, because we are.'

*   *   *

Elizabeth

She's tiny. That's the first thing.

I'm at the Tower of London, where I've brought my mum to meet the Queen, which is rare indeed, and here she is now, coming towards us in the autumn of 2014: Elizabeth Alexandra Mary Windsor, whose official title is Elizabeth the Second, by the Grace of God, of the United Kingdom of Great Britain and Northern Ireland and of Her Other Realms and Territories Queen, Head of the Commonwealth, Defender of the Faith. A huge title for a woman who is tiny, at least physically. Let's call her Lizzie, if we dare. Or Granny. The National Grandmother, five foot four in her prime, but now barely five feet, I would say, looking at her. Here she comes in turquoise, in one of those bright coats that help subjects see the sovereign from far away.

For most of us, most of the time, conversation with the Queen is impossible. She's the Queen. You can camp outside the castle all night if you like, but you're not gonna get a deep chat. However, the survival of the monarchy in a democratic age depends on the common people – that's me and you – feeling a connection with those who rule over them, which is her, and she knows this very well. She also knows her animals. She loves corgis and horses, and emperor stags with their mighty antlers, and understands their kingdom, and knows from them that there's more than one way to connect. And one of those ways is to project, so you can be seen in all your glory. The bright clothes. The regal bearing. The way she waves. (You know the way she waves, you could do it now: arm up at a right angle, hand rotating on the wrist, that's the Queen. That's her trademark. Like the silhouette of her that's on the money. Literally, on the money. You know you're famous when people not only recognise your silhouette, they buy their chips with it.)

This is the most famous woman in the world, as famous as her own country. Displaying herself at public events, in galleries, high up in grandstands, when she's being driven in her big black limo or her golden carriage, or walking among the people, or near them anyway, the tiny granny playing a huge role, dressed to seem much bigger than she is: like a peacock with its feathers wide, or a lizard with its frills unfurled, or that harmless moth, whose wings are patterned in the shape of a pair of eyes and an open mouth, so predators think it's a snake.

Here she comes then, in a turquoise pill-box hat, and a turquoise coat with black trim, clutching a patent black bag, dressed like nobody else ever dresses, in clothes that are intended to hide the lines and frailties of a ninety-year-old body, to bring order and structure, and the appearance of strength, while at the same time looking like something your granny might have worn in the fifties, which is genius.

She's in the room, coming down the line of people who've been put in place to meet her, including me and my mum Marion, who smiles tightly, and I see she's nervous.

The Queen looks super-sleek, her beady, surprisingly playful eyes shining, head nodding slightly at the few fumbled words each star-struck subject is allowed, and the nods remind me of a Muppet, safe and friendly, nodding to affirm what's being said, happily content, but not really there.

'Yes, Ma'am,' says the lady next to me, nearly knocking out the sovereign's eye with a hat feather as she curtsies. (She rhymes it with the start of Marmite, although it should rhyme with jam. My mum told me that.) But wait. What are we doing here?

Well, to answer that I have to tell you a ghost story.

*   *   *

The heavy black iron bolt slid back and the door of my cell for the night opened with a mighty creak, and a dark, strong voice said: 'Good luck then.'

This was the Constable of the Tower of London, the Lord General Sir Richard Dannatt, former head of the British Army, a veteran of many campaigns, someone who'd seen horrors and fought hard, and lost friends, and been in terrible situations that made his blood curdle and his nerves scream, but who now shook me firmly by the hand at the doorway of the cell and said: 'Rather you than me. Nobody has slept in here since Thomas More left to be executed in 1535 . . .'

I stepped inside and there it was: a bare room with sandstone walls and a pitted floor, and arrow slits in the shape of a cross, that let in the cold, but very little light; and a vaulted Norman ceiling that gave this place the feeling of a chapel.

I knew this was considered a sacred space, and that believers fell silent when they entered the cell where the man they called Saint Thomas More had spent his final days, as his former friend the king tried to break his will. The winter he was in here was the fiercest anyone then could remember, and Thomas was broken by it, physically, as damp ghosted into his bones, arthritis bent him double in pain, and he prepared to meet his end.

Lord Dannatt told me Thomas More was an intelligent, articulate man, a scholar and a personal friend of Henry VIII, but he couldn't find a way to support Henry's divorce, or the king's decision to split from Rome and make himself the supreme head of a new Church. 'This was a man who stood up for what he believed, and who was willing to die for it.'

So More was a prisoner of conscience; but real life's never that simple, is it? He persecuted those who had different beliefs from his, possibly tortured them. Six were burned as heretics while he was Lord Chancellor. Lord Dannatt conceded, with military understatement: 'We are not talking about a man whose hands are completely clean.'

When they fell out, Henry tried to teach his friend a lesson. Thomas was locked up but looked after, with wine and furniture and books and writing materials, but as he refused to back down, his privileges were taken away, until he was alone in this bare cell, facing the sentence of death for high treason, which would mean being hanged, drawn and quartered, although Henry changed that to decapitation, which was quicker and less painful. A small act of mercy for a former friend. 'I won't let them put a noose around your neck, cut you down when you're only half strangled, pull out your guts while you're still alive and cut you into quarters. No. I'll tell them to sharpen the axe and make it quick, because I love you.' And I was about to spend the night where Thomas spent the night before that happened, in the lower cell in the Bell Tower, with the Thames lapping outside, down below, and the sounds of people passing by, talking, courting, crying for him, maybe, until the dawn came up on 6 July 1535 and the door of this cell was opened and guards led Thomas More away to Tower Hill, to have his head cut off.

I had a soldier offering kindness. 'There's a bed waiting for you,' said the general, who lived next door. 'When the dawn comes, as far as I'm concerned you will have kept your watch.' Then he left me to it, with a sleeping bag and an open mind, senses overloading, as the sounds of modern London slid through those arrow loops.

I felt chilly, to say the least. There seemed little hope of sleep. And I wanted to do something meaningful, to engage with the place, to respond to its history and listen to its lessons, so I lit a candle. And by the flickering flame I read out loud the words that Thomas wrote here, on the night before he was beheaded. Not on paper but on a scrap of cloth, and not with a pencil or with ink and quill – those had been taken away from him – but with a stub of a stick, charred in the candle flame.

He was writing to his daughter Meg, a brilliant woman, among the smartest of her day, remembering the last time they had seen each other, which was on the day of his sentence, as he walked to the Tower. Meg elbowed her way through the crowd, pushed past the guards, and flung her arms around her dad, and kissed him and kissed him, choked with emotion, unable to say anything, until a soldier ordered her to stop, and forced her roughly away. Thomas had tried to reassure her, she kissed him one more time, then he turned and walked away towards his prison, without looking back. Now, as the moments slipped past and each hacking breath brought him closer to the dawn and to the end, he tried to write something that if she ever saw it would help her, somehow.

Our Lord bless you, my good daughter, and your good husband, and your little boy, and all yours, and all my children, and all my god-children, and all our friends . . . I never liked your manner towards me better, than when you kissed me last . . . farewell, my dear child, and pray for me, and I shall for you, and for all your friends, that we may merrily meet in heaven.

The darkness smothered my face. I lay inside the sleeping bag with the hood around my head trying to order myself to sleep, having blown out the candle, because midnight was long gone, and I would have to work in the morning, but I was wide awake, against my will. Somehow, a connection had been made, through the words of love and the slight flame, and the leap of imagination, back to then, back to him and her; but it wasn't just that, and it wasn't just the rush of adrenaline at being in this place, the first person in hundreds of years to spend the night here. I also had a very real feeling of being watched.

I was so tired, but my body was saying: 'No, you can't sleep, are you joking? There's danger in this place, this is dangerous, wake up, get up, look out!'

I couldn't override this, it was out of my control, like the feeling you must get when your house is on fire. So I sat up and unzipped the bag and flicked on an electric torch, and flooded the corner where I felt my watcher must be, with sweet, revealing light.

There was nobody there. But even in the light, it felt as if there was.

There are lots of alarming stories about ghosts at the Tower: the white lady, the screaming countess, the princes who died in captivity, even a ghostly bear and a sinister smothering force; but this didn't feel like a haunting.

This presence was not frightening, it was not friendly but it was not hostile. I just had the feeling of being observed, by someone with authority and presence, although not Sir Thomas More, I thought then, for some reason. There were plenty of other candidates. And, of course, I could have been making it all up, subconsciously summoning up the feeling, because I wanted something to happen. I'm not ruling that out, but it was so tangible in the moment that I said hello.

'Hello? Hi. You all right?'

I know it sounds strange. There was no reply. I could see nothing, but the feeling was real, and so was the compulsion to explain myself. I was in the Tower in the middle of the night and I felt there was something or somebody there with me; and I was in their place. I felt the need to speak, as you might to a bull in a field.

'Look, I'm so sorry to disturb you, I really mean no harm.'

Was I scared? Yeah, I was. I didn't sleep a wink. As soon as the dawn came I ran off to the general's bed.

*   *   *

The chapel of St Peter ad Vincula, the church inside the Tower of London, is named after the character in the Bible who denied knowing his close friend Jesus three times during his trial, and who went fishing to ease his guilt and grief, to work out the sorrow with his hands, but who saw the ghost of his murdered mate on the shoreline, smiling, and leapt out of the boat and swam and splashed and ran towards the spectre, which turned out to be the real and resurrected man, at least according to the story. That must have been a comfort to Peter, much later, when he was arrested for his love and put in chains, which is what gives the chapel at the Tower its name. And I wonder if Sir Thomas More thought about that story, as he sat in his cell close by to the chapel, because they say an angel appeared to Peter and told him to get up and leave, and the door of his jail swung open, and Peter walked out, no longer in chains; and surely – surely – Sir Thomas More thought: 'If what I'm doing is right, if God is really with me, why can't I be rescued too?'

Instead of which he was executed according to the brutal manners of Tudor England and his head was put on a pike on London Bridge for all to see, as an example; but after a month out there in the open it was rescued by his daughter Meg, who bribed the man who was meant to chuck the head in the river. She kept the head of her father pickled in spices in a jar, until her own death, when the skull was buried beside her.

His body lay headless under the chapel of Saint Peter ad Vincula, near Anne Boleyn, who had pleased and then displeased the king, like Catherine Howard, who was taken as a teenager to be Henry's next wife but killed less than two years later; and Lady Jane Grey, who was named Queen at the age of sixteen but deposed after nine days and executed too; all of them, in their own ways, victims of the Crown.

*   *   *

Lord Dannatt wanted to raise money to restore the chapel and to honour Thomas More, so he asked me to write about it, but I said: 'No, that sounds too dull. Couldn't I do something more interesting instead like spend a night at the Tower?' Because here was a chance to do something extraordinary, to really connect with the spirit of the place, by which I mean not just the look it has, the elegance of the architecture, the faded stone, the scars of battle, the scent of ancient wood, the sounds of voices echoing, the spookiness of a castle at night, but also anything that remains from all that has gone before: from the people who were there, and the stories they told and the stories told about them, and the prayers they sent up in thanks or desperation, the human desire for an answer or a rescue, creating a powerful energy in the room, the sorrow of the doomed, the hope of the devout, the tears of the grieving, the joy of the reprieved, the ecstasy of lovers.

Who knows if these things linger?

Who knows if they bind together in some invisible way, and leave a trace, an atmosphere? Sometimes they seem to.

Sometimes there is a way to sense all that, if you understand where you are and wait quietly, listening, open to anything. And many of us do seem to need to believe that connection like this is possible, if you go to a place and hang about, and try to imagine, as if there's something contagious about it that will touch our own lives and maybe help us.

If someone was good, perhaps we could be good too. That's one of the reasons people waited by the roadside to see Nelson Mandela's coffin pass; it's also partly why people go as pilgrims to ancient places, chapels or stones, cathedral or wells, or mountain-top springs where blessings and healings happened long ago, although there may be no evidence for them except a story passed from mouth to ear to mouth down the years. That's enough. It almost doesn't matter what's true, as long as there is a story we can gather around, to catch some warmth on cold nights; a trace of the divine, a rub of luck or even just a spark of goodness.

There's a shrine on a wall in Cardiff Bay where photographs and poems have been placed in memory of a young man called Ianto Jones. People leave gifts and flowers and write testimonies to the way his life has touched them, as someone who was openly, wonderfully, bravely bisexual, who loved without fear, and died for love. And it's beautiful. It's really moving. When I was there, I saw a couple standing together, arms around each other, reading the cards, with tears on their faces. You can see that lives have been changed by Ianto Jones, but the thing is, he's not real.

He was a character in a science fiction drama on the television called *Torchwood*.

Made up by a writer, embodied by an actor.

A work of fiction. But the change, the love, the sense of community, the sense of belonging that has grown up around him, and the way people have been helped, consoled, inspired, made braver, all of those are real.

So it was with the Queen, while she was still alive. Not Lizzie, the real person, but the part she played, the way we gathered around her image, the story we told, which helped us define ourselves. She was only monarch because we said so and the same applies to her son. Let's be honest, it's all by accident of birth. That could have been me. I could have been king. So could you, or queen. Okay, maybe we were born too late, but my grandmother Gladys was born around the same time as Elizabeth, in the same city. They both served their country during the war: Gladys as a fire warden, climbing to the top of tall buildings during the Blitz to see where the bombs were falling and the flames were rising; Lizzie driving a truck for the Army, learning how to fix the spark plugs, up to her elbows in grease. They both married brave men, Frank and Phil, who went off to fight. Both young women were in the crowds of central London on VE Day, tight among strangers, high with the surge of relief, hidden among the people celebrating, singing, kissing, laughing. They both were full of hope as the fifties came: young and in love and happy. Then Lizzie lost her dad and everything changed, as she'd known it would, partly because her uncle David had set aside the crown for the sake of a woman he loved and partly by sheer cosmic chance. She didn't choose this. She didn't even want it, as far as we know, but she was made Queen. Too young, too young at twenty-five and heavy is the head that wears the crown.

At least she had Phil, while Gladys had Frank. Both men home from war, one in search of a meaningful role, one a printer from the East End who loved his football. And Prince Philip may have been scratchy, and moody, and he may even have strayed, but he also stayed by her side. Two steps behind in public, looking out for her, making sure she was all right. Challenging her in private – arguing, provoking, thrilling, frustrating – the man who knew those most secret parts of her that were hidden from us all.

Let's not romanticise this. Their relationship seems to have been very difficult, but he was there. He was real. She must have needed that, through all the madness.

The way to keep the crown, she'd been taught, was to appear just ordinary enough for the common people to feel a connection, but different enough to be considered royal. And while her children and grandchildren did their best to look as much of a mess as the rest of us, with their catastrophic love lives, fall-outs and failures, tragedies and scandals, Elizabeth somehow managed to remain serene, right up to the time of her death in September 2022. Keeping the royal show on the road for seven decades had been something like a miracle for her, and she had done us all a massive favour too.

I'd rather not have a king or a queen, to be honest. I'd rather live in a country of equals; but even a republican has to admit she was a great one. A constant, calming presence in a nation that so often needed calm; working hard with such a sense of calling, carrying the values of a wartime generation who just kept going through the darkest hours, but who have nearly all gone, like Gladys and Frank and Philip and now Elizabeth. She kept going until the Platinum Jubilee celebrations, making one last appearance on the balcony to wave at the crowds and – on reflection – to say goodbye. I wonder what it was like to be the embodiment of a nation's identity, an idea and an ideal, the centre of a huge wheel that sometimes seemed to be broken and spinning out of control; and to also be someone's granny, someone's mum, someone's sister, someone's widow, her own woman, with her own aches and pains; to wake up in a palace but still have worries in your head and an aching in your heart. I hope she knew she was loved, not just for what she was but for who she was. We all need that. And as we return to the story of the day they nearly met, I can hear my mother's voice saying: 'If anyone had a sense of duty it was her.'

*　　*　　*

Her Majesty the Queen is coming down the line towards us in the autumn of 2014, a year after my night in the cell. The tiny granny with the huge title, in her turquoise hat and turquoise coat with her patent black bag, with the Duke of Edinburgh right by her side, his eyebrows like eagle wings and a quizzical look in his eye.

'What brings you here?'

I mumble some answer about the night in the cell and real- ise my mouth is suddenly incredibly dry and I think: why am I calling him 'sir'? Why am I deferring to this man whose position I don't really believe in? And before I can answer, he's turning to my mum and saying: 'Is this your son?'

And she says: 'Yes, sir.'

And he says: 'Couldn't he think of somewhere better to take you?'

And he's off down the line with his hands clasped behind his back, leaning forward like an inquisitor, and we're both left wondering if he meant it, thinking it must have been a joke, and we agree it must have been and we sort of laugh.

And we realise the Queen has moved on, we've missed her. The Duke was our distraction while she spoke to the impor- tant people.

Then comes the service in the chapel to give thanks for the restoration. In my mind there aren't many of us in there, maybe forty. It feels intimate. I think of the headless bodies of Anne Boleyn and Catherine Howard and Lady Jane Grey beneath our feet and wonder again at the miracle of a woman surviving for seventy years as Queen, a title that has so often been a killer. I can see her in my direct line of sight, close: Elizabeth, the ninety-year-old, who for all the pomp of the surroundings and the splendour of her display still reminds me of Gladys, my nan; and who is as close to me now as Gladys was in the rest home the last time I saw her, when we were all singing 'Bye Bye Blackbird' and I looked across and she smiled. And we stand and sit and stand and sit to sing and to pray, until the moment that is most surreal. Everybody stands to sing 'God Save the Queen'.

'God save our gracious Queen.
Long live our noble Queen . . .'

Elizabeth does not sing this. She sits, with her hands clasped on her lap while we run through the lines she must have heard a million times. They're all about her, but they're not really. They're about the notion of the Queen and I don't see the empress of a lost empire or a symbol of anything in that seat. I see an old lady, who is probably dying to put her feet up and have a cup of tea but who knows her place, who does her duty and has done for so long it must have become habitual and is nodding along to the rhythms of the anthem, in that happy way a Muppet nods, entirely self-contained; until she glances up at her husband and makes eye contact, and maybe he winks, or whatever he does, I don't see, but she smiles, and she has to put her head down to avoid a big old laugh during the national anthem, because that wouldn't look right, would it? The smile lingers.

Honestly, the pair of them. Entirely public, entirely on duty, still themselves.

And outside, afterwards, I loosen my tie and Mum kicks off her shoes for a while on that warm day, and we walk along the walls to look at the poppies: a wave of them spilling out of the Tower and over the stones and across the grass to the moat. *Blood Swept Lands and Seas of Red* this piece of art is called and it is powerful. There are 888,246 ceramic poppies, each one representing a life: a man or a woman, a boy or a girl who died for King and Country in the First World War. The Great War. The War to End All Wars, which it did not. And I think of the parents of all these people who are poppies – the sisters and brothers, friends and lovers – and how it is that love endures.

And I think of Meg with her arms around Sir Thomas More, barely able to let him go; and the couple standing together by the shrine to Ianto Jones; and the smile that lingered on Elizabeth's face; and I realise that to survive in the midst of all this symbolism, all these big ideas and ideals that bind and inspire but also crush and kill, you've got to find something tangible, someone or something real you can trust and hold on to, through it all.

'Hey, Mother, come here,' I say. And out there in the open, in the grounds of the Tower by the flowers of the fallen, I hug my mum and she holds me, tight.

*　　*　　*

Sherry

We've been to palaces, towers and fine hotels, but now we are in a room with a low ceiling. A neon light flickers. A woman sitting across the table from me, a little hunched over and nervous-looking, twists a lanyard in her fingers like a rosary and flicks a glance at the closed door, her lips pursed as if this is some kind of interrogation, a meeting with an official. It's not. I try to let her know that with a smile, by keeping eye contact, leaning closer. Her eyes are clever, inquisitive, wary. We don't know each other, we've never met before and only just been introduced. 'Hello, my name is Sherry,' she says, quietly. 'I am originally from the Philippines and I came here as a domestic worker with diplomats and I've been enslaved as well. I met my husband here and he is also having a lot of problems. I am the main carer in our house. I care for him and I care for our little one as well. He is two and a half.'

No, you're not imagining it, she did just say the word 'enslaved'. I missed it at first, because of all I have seen and heard on the way to meet her, on a short walk across London. Three miles, through some of the richest streets in the world and some of the poorest. Frankly, it's cracked me open.

*   *   *

Let's go back half a day in time and three miles south, to walk through the streets of Knightsbridge in the early morning. A shift change is happening: a security man yawns as he hands over custody of the shop he has paced all night, surrounded by handbags, the price of any one of which

75

would pay his wages for a month. Lorries rush by outside, beating the rush hour. Night workers, blank-faced, wait for the bus – already in their beds, in their heads – and commuters arrive to begin the working day, all part of the silent dance, the state of flux, the changing of the guard that happens without a word or a nod.

I'm straight through the big doors of Harrods, formerly the most prestigious store in the world, once the epitome of posh, before it was turned into a temple of bling. New owners are trying to reverse that process and restore the sense of luxury, so in the Food Hall you can buy a sourdough loaf with your initials baked into the crust for £15. In the fridge with the drinks there's a litre of water – harvested from orphan icebergs in the Arctic, the label says, but still just water – priced at £85.

That's £85, for natural water.

Somebody must be prepared to pay this, but then Harrods is in Kensington, where the seriously wealthy dwell. The average wage among people who live around here is £122,800 a year, three times as much as the national average. A male baby born here can expect to live to ninety-one, which goes to show what decent food and living conditions, good health care and the luck of time and place can do for a boy. I'm heading just a little way north across London after this, to a place where families crowd into rented rooms, men and women struggle to get by on the minimum wage or less, Dickensian diseases like rickets and malnourishment persist, and life expectancy falls to just seventy-six, or a decade lower among certain communities. And I'm wondering, how do we live together? The super-rich and people with nothing – and those of us caught in the middle – side by side.

A Ferrari moves through the traffic, full-throated, glittering gold in the weak autumn sun; shoppers carry Gucci and

Yves Saint Laurent as if the bags are trophies and people look beautiful, well groomed and on display as they sidestep a man in a wheelchair who is calling out from their waist height, wondering if anyone wants to buy the *Big Issue*? He's in his thirties, I guess. Dark hair, street punk clothes, a deeply lined face that cracks into a grin when I ask why he's here: 'More very rich people.' Do they buy from him? 'Some. Buy and go.' And the others? 'Don't see me.'

Whether they are buying or not, whether they are kind and charitable or not, they never really seem to fully notice and acknowledge him, he says. He's the guy in the wheelchair to them, the *Big Issue* seller, the Eastern European with the thick accent. I'm not so sure he sees them either though, because the encounters are brief, they don't want to be seen, they represent the money he needs to make to survive; and if he really stopped for a moment to think about all the wealth that is around him and how much any given individual in front of him really has, it would surely hurt like hell. I know that because I ask him: what about the Ferrari driver? What about that young man behind the wheel in his sunglasses, handsome and apparently happy and maybe worth a million? 'Can't think about it,' he says and looks away. Why not? He winces. 'I would want to kill him.'

*   *   *

There's a Jewish philosopher called Martin Buber who talks about two ways of seeing; in German they are *Es* and *Du*. Let's say 'It' and 'You'. In the first case, if I don't know you and don't want to take the time to know you but think of you in terms of the job you do, the title you hold, the way you look or the clothes you wear, maybe, or the things you can do for me, I'll be treating you as an object. Not 'who' but 'what'. It. I may never even know your name. (And yes, to be honest that is what I just did with the *Big Issue* seller, whose name could have been Clyde or Daniel or Sanjay or Bob, who could have had a PhD in nuclear physics, but to me he was a person struggling, to be contrasted with an apparently smug rich young man, and the source of a good quote, not much more. I'm sorry.)

There's another way of seeing, according to Martin Buber, which is all about opening up to one another: asking, listening, learning, daring to show who we really are, being willing to see the other as they really are too. It's incredibly rare, and difficult to do and risky in the extreme sometimes, but it's worth beginning to try.

For Buber, to see someone as 'You' and not just 'It' was a rare and precious thing that gave a glimpse of the divine. As he put it: 'When two people relate to each other authentically and humanly, God is the electricity that surges between them.'

If there is a god out there – in here, in me, everywhere, present in the natural world in every molecule, glance, touch, laugh and sunset, waiting to be noticed, waiting for us to realise, waiting for us to hear the music that plays behind all things that once heard cannot be unheard – and if we are in some mysterious way, as the ancient texts say, made in the same image, then there is a chance that opening ourselves up to each other without defence or pretence may open us up to sharing the divine. Or as Buber puts it, with reference to the Ten Commandments Moses brought down from the mountain: 'The true meaning of "love one's neighbour" is not that it is a command from God which we are to fulfil, but that through it and in it we meet God.'

I'm not sure how that works, to be honest with you, but I do know life isn't a melodrama: the poor are not all bad and the rich are not all good, we are complicated people, all of us, as I am reminded as I walk on up through Kensington to a room in a private club where a man I know is waiting with a glass of fizzy water in his hand to talk about how he inherited a fortune and gave it all away. He has agreed to help me think about how those who have nothing and those who have everything see each other, on the understanding that he can remain anonymous, which says something in itself. 'It felt like the right thing to do,' says John, who was given £30 million on his twenty-first birthday and put every penny into a charity he did not control. 'It was in the DNA.'

John was the heir to a business empire, the son of parents who were passionate and generous about making the world a better place, who spent millions on good causes themselves, and who supported his decision. All of which sounds ideal, except that John happened to be – in private, secretly – something his parents could not at that time tolerate, because it was against their own, distinct, conservative religious tradition.

'The pressure was intense because I was gay,' he tells me. 'I mean I still am. But being gay in the seventies was not easy. There were no positive role models. For the first ten years of my life, it was actually illegal to be homosexual. I just wanted it to be over, so getting myself obliterated with booze was the best thing.'

He was only too aware of his privilege, to be fair.

'I was living in a gilded cage. I would have been unhappy wherever I was then because I was fundamentally unhappy.'

He chooses his words carefully, this private, cautious man. You wouldn't think he was so wealthy if you saw him in the street, just another middle-aged man in chinos and an open shirt – maybe an off-duty lawyer dressed for comfort, with a haircut that says: 'Just tidy it up a bit, will you?' But the fund he started at twenty-one is now worth £150 million and

John's own personal fortune is not far short of that, because more money came his way in the eighties, through inheritance yes, but also smart investment. Even then, he was mixed up. When I ask him to describe himself in those days, John comes up with three surprising words: 'Defiance, belligerence, entitlement.' He used drink, drugs and male escorts to get him through the days and nights, not seeing those who served him as human.

'I was ruthless in getting my addictive requirements met,' he says. 'If you've got money it is much easier to call up an agency and get a "drug on two legs" as I would call it and objectify another human being, which is something I am not at all comfortable with nowadays. It's an extension of room service. You put it outside the door afterwards, but you pay for it. It's not a way to go on.'

Well, there's a good example of treating another person as an object and not as a human. Martin Buber would be fascinated. It's also a life that sounds very isolating.

'I was incredibly lonely. I realise now why so many wealthy people circulate together, sleep together, whatever. It's about keeping the group closed. We're actually frightened of other people. It's very hard to get to know anyone and not think there's a money element involved in it as well.'

That works both ways, I think. I've known John for a couple of years, since a mutual friend introduced us. I wonder if I should say something about this, then I do: I tell him that it is difficult to know how to be friends with someone when you are only too aware that they could wipe out your mortgage in a moment and barely even notice.

'Yes. I appreciate that. It's not a revelation to me, it's a lived experience.'

His voice is suddenly flat and cold. There goes my chance of a mortgage-free life.

I should say here that John is clean and sober and the many millions he has given away over the decades have done – and do – extraordinary good across the world. I'm reminded suddenly of a scene in *Superman*, where the cries for help from all around the world are so loud the hero is almost paralysed by the overwhelming need. Is it like that for John? 'Yes, and that could be why some wealthy people's response is to shut down and shut it out, because it's just so overwhelming they can't process it.'

John does not believe in quite the same things as his parents did, but he does have a faith of his own that means he can't shut down. I'm still thinking of the *Big Issue* seller though. We both walked past him on the way here. He's not a beggar, he was working for a living, he was keen to let me know that. Also, by the way, his name was George and he was from Romania and he was in a wheelchair because of polio. If John wanted to, he could transform that man's hard life. A thousand pounds would mean little to John but a hell of a lot to George. Is he never tempted to intervene like that?

'No, I'm not a magician.' There's that flat tone again. 'Also it's too obvious, doing something like that. There isn't any discretion in it.' I wonder what he means. John says that if he made one gesture he would feel obliged to get involved and make sure George had a job, a home, the health care he needs. And he can't do that for everyone he meets on the street. 'The clamour is overwhelming. That's why I specialise.'

His charity intervenes in particular communities and goes deep. But I challenge him crudely: in this particular case then, doesn't he want to take responsibility?

'I would actually say I'm not responsible for that individual person. We have the remnants of a safety net in our society for people who are more vulnerable.'

The safety net is failing, I say.

'It used to be a much better safety net, and I believe it will become that again, when people wake up to their social responsibilities and vote accordingly.'

I'm beginning to understand, or at least I think I am: John looks through George as he passes because it would be too complicated and painful to do otherwise; if he gave, he would feel obliged to get involved and there's a safety net anyway, isn't there? And he does his bit already, right? I get that. I use all the same excuses. Still, I insist, he could change George's life in an instant.

'So could you,' he answers.

I'm not rich, I protest.

'Maybe not compared to me,' he says. 'But compared to him? Many people are, including you. So why don't you do it?'

And suddenly I have nothing else to say.

* * *

I'm walking northwards now, past the temples of art, science and learning that are the great Victorian museums of Kensington, then the Royal Albert Hall where Queen Victoria came in 1867, dressed all in black, still grieving for the love of her life who had died six years earlier, saying: 'It has been with a struggle I have nerved myself to be part of today's event.' She was opening in Albert's name a concert hall for the masses, which caused consternation in the letter pages of *The Times*. Somebody wrote a warning that the 'human garbage' of the Strand and Haymarket would now be attracted to the 'comparatively pure atmosphere' of the grand, wide, airy streets of Kensington and Chelsea. They've been keeping us apart a long time.

I'm heading for Sherry, although she's a mile or more away and I don't yet know her name. First I'm meeting a woman called Becky who grew up in Iran before the revolution, when her father was a commercial pilot and life was good, but whose family fled to London when the Shah was deposed and a new, strict religious rule was imposed. Her teenage years were spent in poverty in this foreign land, until she found her own way forward. Becky heard that Puff Daddy was coming to London and would be in a certain club on a certain night, so she scraped together the money for two bottles of his favourite brand of champagne, walked up to him and said: 'I am what you need.'

That must have impressed him because Becky got a job with Puff Daddy. She moved on after a while to become an estate agent, made it to the top of the sales charts in that company then started her own, combining concierge services to the likes of Beyoncé and Jay-Z with selling homes to the super-rich.

'I'm not your typical estate agent,' she says brightly. 'There is, unfortunately, a certain type: white, pinky ring, male, they talk at you and never listen.'

Now she opens the first of many locks on the front door of an apartment that is for sale for £12.5 million, saying that the client has spent a million pounds on the art for the place alone. Don't worry though, there's very tight security and a lot of cameras.

'He's watching you right now,' she says, but I don't know if she's joking.

I'm looking at lemons gleaming in a bowl, all polished and piled up, and Becky says the staff who live here permanently change the lemons at least once a week, so that the place is ready whenever the owner chooses to walk in. If they ever do.

Aren't these places all empty? I've read that one in five is owned by someone who lives overseas, while just down the road there are people living rough, families in tiny flats, kids in deprivation. Becky says yes, but she's a little bit irritated.

'What people don't understand is that my foreign buyers get in a black cab or they go into a restaurant, they stay in hotels, they go to the theatre, they spend money. If you alienate those foreign buyers, the property price might become lower – and you might be able to move in – but you're affecting the economy as a whole. They're just going to stop coming to London and generate another economy in another city.'

Maybe. I'm not convinced by this trickle-down theory, but as we talk I do discover Becky has her limits: 'We don't accommodate people who request a bedroom with no windows for their staff. We just don't deal with them.' I'm sorry? 'They need to find another agent because I think it's disgusting.' Is she serious? 'Yes. When I started my career, domestic staff were being put in the worst compromised positions, their passports taken away from them. I had a flat in Mayfair which had two vaults under the pavement. The family said: "We are going to put the staff in the vaults." I said: "You can't do that, there are no windows." They said: "It's fine, we'll just take the doors out and put bars on the doorways instead, so there's air coming in."' She shakes her head in dismay, even now. 'Bars on the doors. I just said: "I don't want to deal with you."'

Those words are still ringing in my ears as I walk through Kensington Palace Gardens, the richest road in England, with its armed guards, embassies and super-mansions; then up into Notting Hill, past the blue door of the house where Julia Roberts came to stay with Hugh Grant in the movie of the same name, promoting an idealised, Richard Curtis kind of Englishness that attracts tourists even now. And up again to the Portobello Road market with its antiques, record shops and food stalls, wandering off track for a moment to stand in a side street and look up at the blackened hulk of Grenfell Tower, where more than seventy people died in a terrible fire. I'm thinking about how we live in separate bubbles, on social media and in real life, seeing only the people we like and who are like us and only dimly aware of others out there; because although John said it was the rich who huddled together for protection against strangers they did not understand, for fear of having what they had taken away from them, in truth, so many of us are like that. The flames at Grenfell lit up the sky and suddenly it was impossible to ignore your neighbour, rich or poor. Privilege and suffering were illuminated, side by side, and seen by all.

Once you see it, can you really pretend it isn't there? That's a question for us all.

A dozen years ago, a small charity called Trussell Trust was sending out around 40,000 emergency packages a year to people in need. Three days' worth of food at a time, to help them survive. The walk I have been telling you about was undertaken in 2018 for a BBC Radio 4 documentary in which I met George, John, Becky and Sherry; and by then the figure had risen to more than a million emergency packs a year. People were blaming changes to the benefits system as well as a struggling economy. This increase in need happened under a Conservative government – although in the interests of balance I should say that some Conservative MPs thought having so many more food banks was a good thing, an example of great British generosity and compassion. Charity doing what it should, filling in the gaps created by a smaller government that set people free to earn, prosper and help each other. Jacob Rees-Mogg, the millionaire investment banker turned politician, said the rise of food banks to feed those who had no other way of eating was all 'rather uplifting'. The MP for North East Somerset, who lives in a mansion and has two Bentleys, said it 'shows what a compassionate country we are'.

That was before Covid. Before lives were lost and businesses blown apart in the pandemic. Before the war in Ukraine and the energy crisis, before the cost of living began to soar and soar until people who had thought they were doing okay suddenly had to choose between eating and heating. Now things are much worse, the inequalities I saw have become more extreme, the need has gone off the scale. And in the year to March 2022, the Trussell Trust gave away not 40,000 emergency packages but 2.5 million. Half a million more were given out through independent groups, so that's 3 million in total. And now I'm walking under scaffolding on an estate north of Kensington, looking for the room they use as the food bank. It's easy to find: follow the crowd. We are only three miles from Harrods, where people pay £85 for a bottle of water made from orphan Arctic icebergs at a time when a single person is expected to live on that much a week (if they can get their benefits at all), talking to a volunteer who comes in the mornings to help others in need, even though she is going through so much herself.

Sherry, I say, I don't want to pry, but did I hear you right? Did you just say you were enslaved? She looks away and nods. 'I worked for them as a domestic worker. When they came here, they brought me with them. They promised to pay me so much, but when I was here, they paid me only two hundred pounds a month.'

That's nothing. Not enough to live on without the couple who kept her. They were diplomats, working for another country's government.

'They locked me inside the house whenever they went out. Well, it was a flat on the sixth floor. I was locked in every time they go out. I was locked on the sixth floor and I was scared.' No bars on the door then but locks, certainly, both real and psychological. Sherry was terrified of the couple and what they would do to her. They had her passport and allowed her visa to expire and said: 'If you run away, the police will pick you up and deport you and things will be much worse.'

That's how they kept her enslaved, until she saw her chance and found her courage to escape. 'My lady boss lost her key, which meant she could not double-lock the front door any more; she went out and it was not double-locked as usual, so I said to myself: "Maybe it's the time I need to run away from them." I was shaking when I came out, I was very afraid, I did not even realise that I was hardly carrying anything with me, my luggage is just small luggage. I was hurrying, thinking they would catch me,' she says.

'I was really scared. I was down in the lift and out in the street and I didn't know what to do, how to get away so they couldn't find me. I kept thinking: "They're going to be there . . . if I go round the corner I will see them." I was terrified.'

I don't know what happened next. I could slow her down, make her tell the story in more detail, but I don't press her at this point. That would seem too much like an interrogation – too cruel, too intrusive – and she is weeping. Almost weeping. That's what we say for shorthand, but in reality, what is it? Her shoulders are tight and trembling, her eyes are glistening, her voice is a whisper, her breath is shallow, she's twisting and twisting the visitor's card at the end of that lanyard in her fingers and I do not want to distress her any more, so I let Sherry tell this story at her own speed.

'I went to find somebody from the Filipino community. They told me a charity I should go and see, and the charity referred me to a solicitor and now my case is being dealt with by the police; because they are diplomats it is really complicated, there have been lots of interviews, it's still going on even now and I don't have my visa, because when I was working for them my visa had already gone. So, I am not allowed to work. I want to work, but I am not allowed.' I know people like her sometimes have to struggle really hard to convince the authorities that they are for real, but there's something in her eyes, in her body language, in her voice, in her determination to get these words out through the choking filters of her fears, that makes me believe her, absolutely. 'I survived,' she says simply. 'And after a while I met my husband and he helped me a lot.'

She tells me his name but let's call him something else for the sake of his privacy. I have changed her name too, for much the same reason. Ivan is a builder. 'For a while things were good. He was earning and we had some money and we had a child and then things began to go wrong.' Ivan became physically ill and as a result his business failed. 'He was not able to manage because of his health.' He applied for state help but found the system harsh. 'The benefits people asked a lot of questions. They were very tough on us. That's when my husband started to be mentally ill too.'

She pauses, lost in thought, and I wonder about the shadow that just crossed her face, but before I can ask, she speaks.

'We lost another child as well. I had an ectopic pregnancy.'

I'm sorry, I say. That's horrible.

'Thank you,' she says softly. 'He is the one who was more affected by what happened. He doesn't talk. Before, he was so sharp, he was focused on what he did, but since then, when you talk to him, he doesn't respond. We asked for help at the mental team and they did help, but not really: you need to push to get the help you need.'

Ivan is no longer the man she married.

'Yeah, but he's my husband, you know?'

Their benefits were stopped for two months because of a mistake in the paperwork, a glitch in the system, a casual cruelty like so many others that happen but devastating to this particular woman and her family. The people who administer the system don't see her as anything other than a name on the list and the people who are making the policies don't see her either, ever. We learn from each other by trading stories, sharing and listening, seeing how lives are being lived, for real. But in the system, nobody is listening. Nobody is looking. Nobody is hearing or seeing. So, she was forced to come to the food bank.

'The first time I came here, I really cried. I was frightened. I was like: "What's going to happen to us? How are we going to feed our son?"'

And what were the people like in the food bank?

'They treated us like family,' she says. I get the feeling there is no higher compliment that Sherry could give. A few months later, she comes to help out before college, where she is taking classes in English, maths and computer science. 'They helped me and I want to help as well,' she says. 'I'm looking forward to bringing the company back in the future, building it up so I don't need to depend on benefits any more. Ivan has the knowledge in construction, I will do the office work, that's the future. For now, while he's getting better with the support he needs, I'm going to study.'

When a situation is overwhelming, for Sherry or for John the rich man or for Superman, all you can do is do what you can do, one thing at a time. Get through. Love and try. Sherry has nothing to give but herself, but giving herself here helps her. And I can tell from the warmth in her voice, the empathy in her eyes, the courage in her story and the strength in her presence that just by being here Sherry must help a lot of people. She's helping me. I don't really know her, of course. I can't really see her in the way Martin Buber means, not in a short conversation like this which is a transaction: she has been asked by the food bank to tell her story, I want to be able to give some sense of what it's like for her, there's a recording being made, we're both aware it's an artificial situation and when it ends we will both move on, but it's a start, surely?

We've got to make a start, haven't we?

I really admire the way Sherry is refusing to go under in the most challenging circumstances, remaking her own story and reaching out to help others, and I want to learn from her, so I mention this walk I've been on. I tell her that I've seen a lot of people with a lot of money. Really rich people with really huge houses. What does she think of those people? Sherry answers with enormous generosity, more than I could ever manage, but also makes a plea that speaks to us all. 'I hope those people can see what's around them,' she says and that's the point: the seeing and the being seen. 'I know they've worked hard for what they have, they deserve that; but hopefully they also have it in their heart to help.'

*   *   *

Loving

'What we need is a new way of being in the world together that embodies the reality that all life is sacred, precious and connected.'
Richard Rohr

Susan

This is difficult. I am about to interview someone who is genuine Hollywood royalty, as they say, although I daresay she would not be in favour of a monarchy. An Oscar winner for *Dead Man Walking*, a feminist icon for *Thelma & Louise*, a brilliant actor in so much of what she has done and a spiky, persistent campaigner for causes she considers good, who is unafraid to speak her mind or make trouble. An upsetter. An artist and an agitator.

Susan Sarandon, of whom I am a little afraid.

And worse than that, we are doing this on Zoom. The plague has struck again in 2021 and sent us all scurrying to our rooms, staring at screens, talking to pixels all day long; still trying to connect with each other somehow, but actually shouting at ourselves, hoping our voices carry across the ether through the waves of real and imagined haze.

'There's something wrong with the laptop, I'm going to have to use the iPad,' she says from a hotel room in Atlanta, Georgia, thousands of miles away. 'I'll have to hold it like this,' she says, coming into view, then going again.

'Feel free to put it down,' I say. 'We can just talk.'

We don't have to stare into the electronic representation of each other's eyes. It's not ideal, I'd rather be in the room, but at this point I'd also rather have her relaxed and happy; but Susan Sarandon says: 'No. It's all right. I'm an actor, I do well with pain.'

Not real pain, I think. Pretend pain. But I don't say that, because I know she's a human who must have pain in her real life, and not just an actor but a person who regularly speaks up for those who really are in pain, like refugees and exiles and the hungry and homeless. Much more than I do. I'm in my bedroom at home, looking at my own face in one of the windows on screen, wondering if she can see the angry red blemish on my chin. Zoom forces us all to speak to the mirror like the wicked stepmother in *Snow White and the Seven Dwarfs*, wondering, am I fair enough?

* * *

The sun is still high in the sky where she is, although it is the middle of the night here. We were supposed to speak a week ago, when Susan was at home in her apartment in Greenwich Village, but a massive storm hit New York and it was pandemonium. 'There was a lot of flooding,' she says, and that's too true. Hurricane Ida dumped three inches of rain in an hour in early September 2021 and at least thirteen people drowned in their own basement apartments. 'My siblings and their kids lost basements. My son who was in Brooklyn, the place where he was staying, got very flooded and he called me to come take the dog. I said: "I can't come take the dog. We're in the middle, there's no way for me to get there. Call your brother."' She was on the island of Manhattan, across the Hudson, unable to show up for her son this time. 'Then his brother, who was also in Brooklyn, got on a bicycle in the middle of everything and pedalled over, which made me very nervous, but he said the streets were empty and no tree fell on him. So he went over to help his brother get the water out and calm him down.'

Much of the Eastern Seaboard lost power for days, but not Susan in her multi-million pound Manhattan apartment. 'We were lucky. In New Jersey, where one of my sisters is, they didn't have power for a very long time because everything's above ground. Restaurants and houses were exploding because of some kind of electrical thing, or gas, I don't know why.' It was just like a disaster movie and a sign of catastrophe to come. 'I don't remember this happening before, where you really can't count on anything,' she says, as someone who has tried to raise the alarm about the real harm climate change is doing to us right now. 'There's hurricanes in places that never had hurricanes, tornadoes in New Jersey. So your brain can't construct a plan.'

The storm blew over this time, so she's down south, on the road, making a drama about country music, doing this interview with me for a British magazine, the point of which is to celebrate her birthday. Susan Sarandon is seventy-five.

'I have a complete disconnect with it,' she says, as disconnection starts to become the theme of this conversation. So do I just now too: looking at her face, framed by fashionable, big, black-rimmed glasses and the familiar tumbledown red curls, you'd think she was at least a decade younger. 'I'm not old. I don't feel seventy-five. It's crazy. Honestly, I'm happy I made it to seventy-five, because I know there are a lot of people that have been less lucky. Physically, I have been getting signals that I'm not twenty-five and I have accepted that,' she says. 'Mentally, it's a strange thing. I have about as much ability to comprehend somebody walking on the moon as I do the fact I'm actually seventy-five.'

She's sitting on the edge of her bed in that faraway hotel room, far away from home even for her, in a white T-shirt top that has gold or yellow bands, it's hard to tell through the screen, as she talks in that gritty drawl of hers – nasal and edgy and yet somehow attractive – that seems to say she knows all about the bull and the injustice thank you, but still crackles with life and is up for anything. I've watched her on a screen so many times, but this is different: she's actually here (or a version of here) being herself (or a version of herself) and she's generous, I think. Some actors I know would be giving one-word answers, declining to talk about their age, but she's happily telling me her secrets, such as they are. 'First of all, you do not smoke. A joint now and then is fine, but not cigarettes. I drink a lot of water. I do yoga. I try to do it at least once a week. I'm very lucky to live in New York so I'm walking all the time. I have to thank my mum for her bone structure. That's all I can say. All my tattoos are in places that won't sag.'

And now she's even showing me birds on her arms, one of which is escaping from a cage, and Susan says there are letters and symbols all down her back which stand for her children and grandchildren. 'If I had realised how much they hurt, I definitely would've made them smaller,' she says. 'I didn't start getting them until I was sixty. There wasn't really anything I wanted to say and then I just decided: Okay.'

I wonder if she feels liberated by her age? Some people do. Susan Sarandon runs her fingers through her hair and smiles. 'If ever I was going to burn bridges it should be now. What, at this point, do I have to lose? So that is freeing. At this point, I don't give a fuck.'

Apologies for the language. It's what she said. Perhaps a little context would help. There have certainly been times when Susan's peers have baulked at her strong views. She was banned from the Oscar ceremony in 1993 for using the stage to protest against Haitians with AIDS being held at Guantánamo Bay; but they had to lift that a couple of years later when she won Best Actress for playing a nun befriending Sean Penn's death row inmate in *Dead Man Walking*. Liberal Hollywood was probably okay with her campaigning to end the death penalty on the back of that picture, maybe even cheering when she opposed the war in Iraq and spoke up against racism and homophobia in cinema, but protesting against bankers on Wall Street? Calling Pope Benedict a Nazi? Refusing to back Hillary Clinton against Trump? These made her enemies; and, actually, that does seem to matter to her.

'Every film I do I see as a love story, because people have the audacity and the courage to reach out to other people, to see and be seen, whoever they are. I'm interested in our human connection. So for me, the most difficult times have been when I've been ostracised and cut off from my tribe and the loneliness of that.'

I know: she must be worth a fortune and it's hard to feel sorry for someone whose shelves groan with awards; but there's no doubt how much it costs to speak out about the so-called wrong things in an industry that considers its own opinions unassailably right. Now, though, it seems she is ready to be even less careful than before. 'My kids are stable and grown and don't need my protection as much, they will not be as damaged now as they were when they were little if stuff comes out in the paper attacking me or people make threats. That was very painful then, because I was thinking about them and not just myself. Now I feel like they're grown-ups, they'll deal with it.'

Does she feel this new freedom in the rest of her life too?

'Yeah. And also, I do think about death a lot more than I did. It seems like every single acting part I get, I'm dying!' She laughs, a raw, ironic, happy sound. 'Every single script, I'm either dying, I have Alzheimer's or I'm helping someone die. That's my oeuvre at this point. But that's a healthy thing, to have to think about all that.'

We're going deep, already.

✻   ✻   ✻

Susan was born in Queens, New York, in 1946, the first of nine children her mother Lenora would have with Philip Tomalin, a television producer. Lenora was from Italy. Susan was raised a Catholic, she went to a Catholic university, so does she have any faith of her own left?

'I really wish I did. I wish I thought that. I know energy can't be destroyed and so there could be some kind of energy that I have that can still be around.' There's a pause while she considers. 'I do not put my trust in being reunited with my deceased family members or friends, no, not really; but my DNA is out there in my kids and grandkids and that's enough.' Is it though? Really? 'I think you have to live by the idea that what you put out in the world, you reap. In that sense, you have an immortality.'

Then there are the movies. If you appear on film and people like what you do then you can live forever, or at least appear to. Susan Sarandon will always be suspended in mid-air above the Grand Canyon in a blue 1966 Thunderbird, one hand on the wheel and one holding the hand of Geena Davis, their eyes locked on each other, smiling, forever flying, never dying. That's the final scene of her biggest film *Thelma & Louise*, as the two women choose to make their own decisions and take their own spectacular way out of being pursued by the Feds after killing a would-be rapist. We were supposed to watch them crash down onto the rocks below, dying in the wreckage and the flames, but the director thought that was too bleak, so the movie ends with a freeze-frame of the car in the air, fading to white. Sure, we know what happens next, the laws of gravity predict it, but the laws of storytelling allow us to stop just at the moment of great change; and the human craving for hope allows us to imagine our own alternative ending, something to hang on to if we need to. And many of us do. The film critic

Manohla Dargis suggests the bond between the two women transcends reality: 'No matter where their trip finally ends, Thelma and Louise have reinvented sisterhood for the American screen.'

Maybe. They still die, though.

The movie was hailed as a breakthrough in the way women are depicted back in 1991, but Susan frowns at this idea. 'The *Thelma & Louise* thing has never broken through. They thought there would be so many more women-led films after we did it and I don't think that happened, but there definitely is a demand.' Thirty years later, with their eyes locked on each other, Thelma and Louise are still flying.

*   *   *

Susan got into all this by accident. She was married to a fellow drama student called Chris Sarandon at the age of twenty and went along to support him when he was called to an audition with an agent. To the great surprise of both of them, the agent saw something in her and asked Susan to try out for a film called *Joe*, which was about a construction worker going on the rampage against hippies, because he thought they were destroying America.

'That was everybody's nightmare at the time, so it became the *Easy Rider* of that year,' she says. 'It's a pretty terrible film.'

Still, it was her breakthrough. Soap operas came next, then a Broadway play and the naive Janet in the movie of *The Rocky Horror Picture Show*, in which she was absolutely terrific. Suddenly Susan was a proper actor. 'I was like: "God, this is what I do now."'

She kept going, kept her surname after divorcing Chris in 1979 and won her first Oscar nomination two years later for *Atlantic City*. And after that? *The Hunger*.

This is the film I am longing to discuss with her the most, because it meant so very much to me when it came out in 1983. It's also the reason she pops up at this point in our overall narrative. I have told you stories about people who are regarded as icons and now, for a while, I would like to talk about those who have influenced me personally, one way or another, for better or worse. I admire Susan Sarandon's determination to use her fame to further the causes that matter most to her; and no movie had more impact than *The Hunger* on my teenage years, a time when we all look for clues as to how to live.

Let's be honest, not everybody thinks *The Hunger* is a classic. The plot does fall apart. The critic Roger Ebert said it was 'agonisingly bad'. But he was not a fifteen-year-old fledgling Goth walking the streets of East London, getting stared at for having black nails and mascara, dodging the thugs to slide into the Walthamstow Granada, sitting on his own in that massive fleapit and watching *The Hunger*. I was and I bloody loved it. The opening scene was electrifying, as the band Bauhaus played their clattering epic 'Bela Lugosi's Dead', their lead singer Peter Murphy staring into the camera, performing in a cage at a nightclub, looking dark and sleek and vulpine sexy and I wanted to be him. So much. But not as much as I wanted to be the man he wanted to be: David Bowie, who appears in that opening scene too, dressed in black, with artificially black hair and black sunglasses, alongside an elegant, rather glacial woman who is smoking and inspecting the dancers, and who happens to be played by Catherine Deneuve, the ice queen of French cinema. The pair of them are drop-dead gorgeous, even as they flirt with a younger man and woman in the nightclub, take them home in a car and brutally, savagely murder them with ancient Egyptian blades, then drink their blood.

Yes, it's a vampire movie. A Gothic lesbian vampire movie to be precise; but one that defies all the expectations and conventions associated with that kind of film until then. It's stylish, the clothes are beautiful, the interiors are to die for, the cheekbones are as sharp as they come, and I was sitting in the dark, soaking it all up as if *The Hunger* was a message from the style gods. You can see its influence in so much that came after, and for a boy who had no internet to help him, who devoured every interview with Bowie to see what he should read and listen to and watch and talk about and be like, this was holy inspiration.

There was something else too, stirring in the shadows, because I was wondering who to love. Bowie made me feel. He made me feel I could be like my friends who were into boys and whose company I adored, whose life and laughter and wicked humour and secret energy sustained me, whose sweaty bodies swept around mine on dance floors in clubs with locked doors and bars on the windows and who were in danger of being beaten up every night and every day, on the streets and in school, and sometimes at home. And all of us, whatever or however confused our sexuality, were drawn to Bowie. All of us looked up to him, like a maverick older brother who dared to do the things we did not dare to do. I was in love with his grace and beauty and mystery and his sense of danger. We all were.

*   *   *

I tell Susan Sarandon I saw *The Hunger* three times in a week when it came out because I thought David Bowie was the coolest human alive and she says, quickly and wistfully: 'You're right. You're totally right.'

And then I remember. Oh, crikey, didn't she have a thing with him? There's a pause while Susan considers whether to answer at all and then she just says, softly: 'Yeah.'

Actually, it was very serious indeed. Susan said nothing of their love at all in public until just a few years ago, and even then it was only a hint dropped in passing. Lots of people got ridiculously excited, though. She and Bowie were two of the most mesmerising performers of their generation; they mean an awful lot to people apart, so the idea of them together blew some minds. 'He's worth idolising. He's extraordinary,' she told a reporter, before hinting at a reason why it ended. 'That was a really interesting period. I wasn't supposed to have kids. I'm the oldest of nine and had mothered all of them, so I wasn't ever in a mode where I was looking to settle down and raise a family . . .'

The implication was that they parted because David wanted children and she did not, but as we talk now I discover that the situation was more complicated than that. Susan had been diagnosed with endometriosis during the making of *The Hunger*. The doctors had prescribed strong drugs to stop her periods being agony and said there would be no kids in the future without surgery. 'I wasn't desperate to have children,' she tells me, having done much of the cooking, cleaning and caring for her siblings when they were young and she was still growing up. 'I felt I had been a mum for quite a while. So when I was told I couldn't do it without operations I thought: "That's okay." I never felt that was what I needed to complete me. So I went years without using birth control.'

Susan was more than a little shocked then when she fell pregnant by the Italian film director Franco Amurri a couple of years after being told it would never happen. She gave birth to a daughter called Eva, and welcomed the sudden change in direction. 'That was a time in my life when I felt really overqualified for all the parts I was getting. Moviemaking had been demystified for me and I thought:

"Maybe I should really become an aid worker." I went to Nicaragua and was getting deeper and deeper into that, then all of a sudden I was pregnant. I was like: "Wow. That's a miracle. I guess I can't be overqualified for this."'

Her sons Jack and Miles were born in 1989 and 1992, when Susan was with the actor and director Tim Robbins, who would be her partner for twenty years. So what of Bowie? The parting sounds painful, but were they ever reconciled? They were nearly neighbours in Greenwich Village in his final years, after all.

'Yeah,' she says again, perhaps wondering whether to talk about this further or not. She never has before. 'Not that we hung out a lot and he had a number of health issues to deal with, but yeah we did. I was fortunate enough to be closer to him right before he died, the last couple of months. He did find me again. We talked to each other and said some things that needed to be said. I was so fortunate to be able to see him, when he told me what was going on with him,' she says, her voice cracking with emotion. 'I love Iman, his wife, someone who was so equal in stature. That was clearly who he was destined to be with. I was so happy she was with him through all of that. I've kept in touch with her a little bit. The last time I saw him was at the premiere of the musical that he did.'

Lazarus, I say, and she agrees. They were photographed together at the event in New York in December 2015. After that she went abroad as part of her campaigning, this time in support of refugees. 'I was in Lesbos to see what was going on there and record interviews with the people. That was probably the toughest thing I've ever done: a never-ending stream of desperation that had no recourse and no way to fix it. The camps were just horrific,' she says. 'It was so disturbing so I wasn't sleeping and I knew that I had to get up early to start meeting the boats as they came in so I took some Ambien, a pretty strong sleep aid. And I had this dream that David had called me and that I'd had this conversation with him and as I hung up I had thought in the dream: "Nobody's going to believe me that David Bowie called me in Lesbos." '

She woke up, marvelled at how vivid the dream had been, then got on with her day.

'Three days later, I thought: "Did he actually call me?" And I went to my phone and he had called me. And I have no recollection of what that conversation was. He died a week later.' She still sounds shocked and hurt that he went. 'That was so frustrating, because I was like: "Oh my God, what was that conversation?" I have no idea.' So, did she never speak to him again? 'No, because I was still in Lesbos. Then I got back.'

Her voice softens to a burr.

'There was a double rainbow in New York on the day that David passed.'

*   *   *

The Hunger is an allegory for AIDS, which was sweeping through New York and San Francisco at the time, silently, because of shame. The ancient vampire Miriam, played by Catherine Deneuve, has bestowed what looks like eternal youth upon her lover John, played by Bowie, but suddenly he begins to age insanely fast because of what feels like a fire in his blood. He turns for help to Susan Sarandon, playing a doctor called Sarah who specialises in ageing, then John disappears. The doctor comes looking for him at Miriam's elegant townhouse, unaware that John is now hidden in the basement with the rest of the vampire's undead former lovers. So with a third of the movie to go its biggest star is locked in a box and turning to dust, because the story is really about these two women, Miriam and Sarah, who have plenty to say and do without any need for a man.

The Hunger was daring for its time, showing same-sex attraction between two women in a relatively dignified way. It is a bit cheesy: there are curtains billowing and candles flickering and delicate piano music plays as they flirt and circle each other and one thing leads to another; but this was the eighties and that's pretty much what the director would have given us if it had been a man and a woman making love, so fair enough. It's also quietly beautiful.

Susan says it could have been much worse. 'The scene was described in the script in a very *Playboy* way,' says Susan, pointing out that it was originally written and directed by two men. 'For me, the most interesting thing if I see a scene that involves intimacy is the beginning and the after, because there's not much difference in what happens in the middle, except the way you shoot it. It's what gets them into bed. So what I ask is: "When did they first touch?" That was something that we created on the spot. I spill my wine, she goes to exchange the shirt and then we hold hands and then we kiss and then the rest of it.'

I love the fact that Susan Sarandon is describing a scene that was seared into my brain at the age of fifteen, the cause of yet more longing in the stalls at the Walthamstow Granada. I know it well, I say. She laughs, presumably at the look on my face. I'm such a fan of this film I have listened to the director's commentary on it and I thought he said body doubles were used, but Susan says no. 'It was us. The first day, everybody was all excited and hanging out in the rafters to watch. By the third day, everyone was bored to tears.'

*　　*　　*

Inevitably, really, given how ground-breaking *The Hunger* and *Thelma & Louise* and other movies of hers were, and as a long-standing ally of LGBTQ+ people, Susan Sarandon gets asked about her own sexuality from time to time. She always seems to try to answer honestly. 'It's up for grabs,' she said a few years ago, after playing Betty Grable in a film called *Feud*, adding that yes, she was open to the idea of dating a woman. I wonder though if it's really true, given that she was asked the question by *Pride Source* magazine, or whether it was just the sort of thing she felt she had to say?

'Yeah. I'm single but open to persuasion, but busy as hell and with lots of wonderful friends and grandchildren and everything. I think everybody is somewhere on a spectrum and I like the fluidity of this now,' she says, meaning the times we live in. 'For me, it's all about connection, curiosity, passion. I had a gay boyfriend who had never been with another woman and we had a very good, fairly long run and it was sexual.'

So has she dated women? 'I think women are beautiful, their bodies are amazing, but for me to open that window I would have to have some kind of connection and there just hasn't been an instance where that crossed my path. I'm not really looking. I feel fulfilled and pretty happy. I would like a travelling companion of some kind, an adventurous soul, but no one's even travelling now so that's on the back-burner. If it's going to happen, it's going to happen. In the meantime, I am dancing in my kitchen.'

*   *   *

What does all this amount to in the end? Two people in long-distance conversation, on opposite sides of the Atlantic, with little more to go on than what the computer gives us, the cues we get from tone of voice, the ideas we are fast forming of each other. I can't tell if she's falling for my frantic attempts to seem friendly, likeable and on her side. I feel the Bowie thing has opened up a truth and connection between us, but I've no idea if that's real. I suppose what I'm experiencing is that even in the most dislocated circumstances, humans keep trying to connect anyway, because we need it, even in the toughest times or the fiercest storms. Connecting with other people is good for us: the doctors say it can help us handle our emotions, feel better about ourselves, develop more empathy, lower anxiety and provide some defence against depression. 'We have a human need for companionship and for close contact,' says the physician and therapist Dr Gabor Maté. 'To be loved, to be attached to, to be accepted, to be seen, to be received for who we are.'

The neuroscientist Professor Matthew Lieberman says connection is as important as the basic need for food, water, shelter and warmth. 'Being socially connected is our brain's lifelong passion. It's been baked into our operating system for tens of millions of years.'

Making connection with someone is easier if you're in the room, the signals are easier to read and respond to, but what about on Zoom? How do you reach out then? How has it happened this time, apparently against the odds? Well, I wonder if for some people, at certain moments in their life, it is actually easier to talk freely on Zoom. They're in their own room, in control of their own space. They can switch off the computer if they want to, or just the camera. They don't have to keep up eye contact, they can look wherever they want, so that maybe when a thought grabs them and they run with it they feel as though they are talking to themselves. Maybe that frees them up, sometimes.

I wasn't trying to trick Susan into talking about David Bowie, I didn't realise she would. I was just sharing my own genuine feelings about him, indulging myself but also reaching out, because beyond my need to get a good quote and her need to publicise whatever it was she was doing next, we were just two humans sharing stories, and that's where it gets really interesting. So maybe it was just that she really wanted to say something about him that had been on her mind and found for a change that here was someone who just might get it, who shared a little of her great love for him and was willing to ask and willing to listen. So she was willing to risk talking.

'You have to do the best you can with what you have,' she says. 'I tell my kids to be authentic and kind. Injustice has always really disturbed me, I don't know why, but from the time I was little I was rotating my dolls' dresses in case they came to life at midnight so one wouldn't have all the good dresses all the time. So that's just a character flaw. And so it's hard to be like that right now.'

I'm struck by her willingness to say things that might on the face of it sound a bit ridiculous and which could be ridiculed but actually seem to reveal someone trying to be true to herself, to give what she can, give all to the moment, take a risk whatever the consequences and somehow, maybe, like Thelma and Louise, fly.

Preferably without dying.

*   *   *

Then something happens as we come to the end of our time that really does feel like connection. Susan wants to read out a quote from the writer Howard Zinn that sums up how she feels about life right now and tears begin to well up.

'"To be hopeful in bad times is not just foolishly romantic. It is based on the fact that human history is a history not only of cruelty but also of compassion, sacrifice, courage, and kindness . . ."' I can see that she is weeping as the last sentence comes. '"To live now as we think human beings should live in defiance of all that's bad around us is itself a marvellous victory."' I try to console her by saying she's clearly tried her best to make the world a better place, as an activist, but also as an actor whose movies have changed the way people think and feel. 'Thank you,' says Susan Sarandon as we come to a quiet but hopeful end. 'That will be a good epitaph: "She gave it her best shot." I think that's all you can ask for. Show up. Just show up.'

*   *   *

Sharon

I was hanging around with a friend called Sharon when *The Hunger* came out. She lived a mile or so from me, down beside the wild, mysterious part of Stratford that was all scrapyards, dodgy lock-ups and falling-down factories. The sort of place where a gang of villains would get cornered in *The Sweeney*. I rode my bike there in the summer just to see what I could find. I wish I could say it was a Chopper, they were very fashionable, but it was a big, heavy green thing my grandad had been given as a postman. Sharon had a council house right by the railway yards with her mum, who never let her go anywhere. Sharon also had cerebral palsy. She could walk fast enough and boy could she talk, but when I knew her as a teenager she had never even been to the West End, even though it was only twenty minutes away on the tube. Her mum would not take her and she certainly would not let Sharon go on her own. The world was deemed too hostile. And not surprisingly, in those days, Sharon didn't have the confidence to challenge this, not until she started to push the boundaries. This began one night at the Lee Valley Ice Rink, which is still there, almost within the boundaries of what became the Olympic Park. Back then it was new and best known for a rowdy Saturday night disco on ice. We went as a group of friends and we were almost in the door when Sharon was refused entry. The bouncer talked to us and not her: 'No, she's not coming in. She can't skate.'

Sharon was angry, as you might imagine. 'I can do it!' she shouted, but the bouncer would not yield. We quickly said that half of us would skate and half would watch from the side of the rink with her. That was fine by me, I've never been a fan of falling over. Sharon accepted her fate reluctantly and said: 'I'll just have a drink.'

The bouncer frowned and crossed his arms. Looking at us and not Sharon, yet again, he said: 'No. I'm not letting her in.'

'Why not?'

'She'll put everyone else off.'

Then there was real anger, voices were raised and a scene was made, but in the end we walked away. We just couldn't win.

*   *   *

I thought of her again in another moment of high emotion, in the summer of 2012, as I stood in a stadium built not far from the ice rink and shouted along with my children to support British athletes at the Paralympics. They were following on from the Olympics, with the team wearing the same kits, representing their country in the same way, and this was a 400-metre race in the T38 class, for people with cerebral palsy, like Sharon. I wondered if she was there. I would have loved to know what she made of the sights and sounds and the spirit of the place that night, the roars of approval as men and women with her condition were passionately and joyfully cheered on by the huge crowd, so close to the scene of her attempted humiliation all those years before. Well, one of them. Sharon was mixed race and differently abled, so she was sadly used to being shouted at in the street in those days and even spat upon. Few people ever listened to what she shouted after them, which was a shame because she was very funny. We lost touch in the way teenagers do, but as I listened to the crowd at London 2012 I thought of all the crap she had endured back then and hoped she was enjoying the way those Olympics and Paralympics were consciously celebrating a new kind of diverse, inclusive Britishness. I guessed it wasn't going to fix the problems of the world, that people who were seen as different would continue to be treated with cruelty and disregard and that the system would continue to be crushing at times to those labelled as disabled; but I also knew that I was seeing Paralympians embraced as heroes in the same way as Olympians, maybe even more so. That had to mean something.

'I hope you are seeing all this, Sharon,' I thought as another race was won. 'I hope you are here in the stadium, in our old manor, watching, cheering, yelling, taking all this in. And I hope that old bastard of a bouncer is too.'

* * *

Mohamed

The noise is incredible. Sixty thousand humans screaming, bellowing, shrieking, pleading with the skies in favour of the one man, all willing him to win. Throw in the roar of a jet engine taking off, jungle beasts in the night, migrating birds and the crash of waves and you have some idea of the extraordinary sound being generated by the crowd in the new stadium at the Olympic Games of 2012 as the 5,000-metres race reaches a climax and the home hero has a chance to win. It's hard to think, hard even to breathe, but who can breathe right now? Everyone is breathless, on their feet or on their toes, looking down into the arena at the orange track encircling a field of green, all bright and shining under floodlights; and fifteen figures moving fast through the iridescence, tight together as if fleeing a common foe; but all eyes are on the one in the white vest and blue shorts, a slender man with a sloping gait, who is quite possibly the greatest British athlete of all time and is now attempting to prove that is true, at the finale of the sporting event of the century, in this country anyway, a show so huge we've run out of hyperbole.

Everybody knows, or thinks they know, the story of Mohamed Farah, born in Somalia twenty-nine years ago, taken to Djibouti to escape the chaos of a civil war, then brought to London to be with his father at the age of eight. He barely spoke a word of English at first, but grew up in West London, playing, laughing, learning, dreaming of becoming a car mechanic or playing for Arsenal, working in

McDonald's instead but running and running and running and winning school title after school title until he was getting help with training, becoming a British citizen and working his way without knowing it towards this moment: the here and now, the climax of a golden summer. We've learned to call him Mo, this spark in a fire of pride and optimism; and here he is now, as the Olympic Games approach their end, still holding the hopes of a nation in his metronomic heart, down there in the centre of the light, steady in the middle of a fight. The running pack is tight. There are fears the others will gang up on him, crowd him out, do whatever it takes to deny him a second gold medal, but that's patriotic paranoia. They're just out to win, as much as he is. And they are some of the finest runners ever to glide across long distances. These runners are going slowly by their own standards, as the stadium commentator says, and they do make it look effortless, but as they come around the bend and down the straight and past the press seats where I'm sitting, they are flying.

Mo has been at the back, worrying those who have not seen him before, but I just saw a wise mum away to my left lean over and shout in the ear of a panicking dad: 'It's okay, Mo knows what he's doing.' And we hope so, as the message is passed on to their kid.

We really hope so, we mums and dads and sons and daughters, we flag-wavers and bearers of home-made placards, we chanters and screamers, we jumpers and shufflers, the overexcited and the playing-it-cool types, and those dizzy from the noise and the ones who are dazed by the head-spinning intensity of this moment.

I'm trying to think of words to write for my report, trying to focus and get this right, knowing I will have to press send as soon as the race ends, hoping my nerve won't go, telling myself: 'Say what you see, say what you see, write that down.'

And Mo is in the middle with a mile to go, but then he moves up the field again as they take another bend and the screams come harder, faster, higher and I see what they're doing; I see it now and marvel. A Mexican wave in the crowd, of course, as we've seen so often here: a great sweep of human movement as people rise up in turn around the stadium, raise their hands in salute then sit down again to watch the wave sweep on. But this one's different: at the top of the wave as they stand they call out his name and bow down and stretch out their hands towards Mo, in the gesture from the movie *Wayne's World* which says: 'We are not worthy.' But there's more, because this is done with a strange, supernatural sense of collective timing, so the rise and the fall and the call are always just ahead of Mo as he runs, and the energy it creates seems to pull him forward at an ever-greater speed, like we're doing it with him; so when the bell rings for the final lap and Mo is in second place we know he'll go. And so he does: up to first. He's leading, with the pride of Kenya and Ethiopia in his wake, and they're all flat out. They've been running for a dozen minutes but this is a sprint finish, and Mo has the energy he needs.

He's all out now, crossing the line a winner, looking astonished, eyes and arms open wide as if he can't believe it. We can't believe it. And the noise? The noise is incredible. I've see and heard the loudest rock bands in the world and witnessed winning goals at massive stadiums, but I've never experienced anything like this or felt anything like the collective release. 'What a race! What a race! What a man!' The reporter next to me is yelling her head off, punching the air. She's from Estonia. It doesn't seem to matter.

Mo's wife is down at the front, heavily pregnant with twins – and heaven only knows how she doesn't have them right here and now. Jamaican athletes in tracksuits are laughing down beside her, because their leader Usain Bolt did press-ups after smashing the 200-metre sprint record and now Mo is sitting on the track doing sit-ups to match his mate's joke after the race of his life. And in comes the thunder of a song we've heard so many times now at these Olympic Games, David Bowie singing how we can be heroes. How strange to hear his howl of anguish, captured in a studio by the Berlin Wall at the height of the Cold War, used as a rallying cry for British athletes; and yet it makes sense in this summer of transformation. Muslims are terrorists, the British have been told falsely, subliminally, explicitly, since 9/11 and 7/7, but here is a British Muslim kneeling to kiss the track, raising his hands to Allah while the crowd continues to chant his name. Seconds later, he is trotting along the perimeter high-fiving kids, posing for pictures, being showered with love while wrapped in the union flag. We are being remade.

*   *   *

The hatred and the fear won't go away, things will get worse in some ways, but maybe this hero worship will help redefine what it means to be us. I go down to the dark, tight rooms under the stands to wait for the press conference and when Mo enters in his muted blue tracksuit designed by Stella McCartney there is spontaneous applause from reporters of all nations, which becomes a standing ovation. 'The crowd was inspiring for sure,' he says. 'If it wasn't for them, you know, I don't think I would have dug in so deep. It just got louder and louder and louder. It reminded me of when you go to a football match and somebody scores a goal. That's how loud it was. I just thought: "Wow."'

*   *   *

This is not just a story about Sir Mohamed Farah and it's not just about sport or even the Olympic Games: it's about the best and the worst of us, so here goes with a change of pace that would make a runner proud. Seven years earlier, on the other side of London, a doctor who had just turned forty was watching the news before work. Dr Andrew Hartle watched a news clip from the previous day, in which the president of the International Olympic Committee opened an envelope to reveal the results of a vote and said: 'The Games of the 30th Olympiad in 2012 are awarded to the city of London.' Cue pandemonium on the London bid tables in Singapore in this clip, with papers flying in celebration and people dancing on the desks in joy. 'I'm ecstatic, absolutely ecstatic,' said the bid leader Sebastian Coe, a former gold medallist who was now a Lord. Winning the bid for the Olympics was seen as a way to unlock billions of pounds, to bring London back to its best even as it struggled with inequality and poverty and the tensions of a world in which the West was at war with a distortion of Islam. Dr Hartle turned off the television and left his flat, walking to work at St Mary's Hospital, Paddington, where he was an anaesthetist.

He said: 'We had not started our list when the cardiac arrest bleeper held by the trainee who was with me went off, saying "Major incident". I went straight down to the A&E resuscitation unit. The news reports were talking about power surges, but one of the consultants mentioned bombs. That just sent a chill.'

Dr Hartle had trained for emergencies such as this but the reality was harder to cope with. 'The image frozen in my mind is of the first patient who came to us, about an hour after the bomb. A patient whose age I couldn't even guess, with probably the most devastating injuries I had seen in my career. Terrible limb injuries and internal injuries. He was blackened by a mixture of smoke and soot and the dirt of being blown out of a tube train underground. He was going to lose both his legs.'

The man had been travelling on the Circle Line between Edgware Road and Paddington when a bomb had gone off in his carriage. Six people had been killed on that train, including the bomber. The paramedic who had brought the first patient in was somebody Dr Hartle knew. 'There was a look on his face I had never seen before. I can't describe it. He was covered in soot and dirt, red in the face and soaking with sweat. It was obvious that what he had seen was something different, something catastrophic.'

The stench was powerful. 'The patients stank of burning smoke.'

The patient was taken away to the operating theatre.

'When the bay was emptied a scene of carnage remained. There was blood and dirt and clothes and stuff everywhere. One thing I remember clearly is the cleaner turning up with his bucket and just getting on with it. That is how it was. There were no arguments like there might be on a normal day, just a common purpose.'

In times of crisis, humans work together. The survival instinct kicks in and while for some that means fight or flight, for others it is tend and befriend. Act collectively. Care for the sick and injured. Work hard, forget yourself, become part of the group, shake off your fears and screaming worries and focus on what's in front of you, the person who needs your help. Do that. Hold their hand. Wipe their face. Treat them as you can, be aware of what's going on around you and give whatever help is possible, because together there is a chance some or many of us might just get through this. Together there is hope.

Dr Hartle would recall in years to come that the hospital was suddenly full of police dressed in black carrying heavy machine guns, giving instructions. 'Anything that came off patients had to be put into paper sacks as evidence. Clothes or shrapnel. Or limbs.'

Thirty-eight patients were brought in to St Mary's that morning, but across the capital there were more than seven hundred injuries.

'London was eerily silent,' Dr Hartle told me in an interview. 'I had got off the tube at Edgware Road every other morning that week at ten to nine, which was the exact time when the bomb went off. The day it happened was the first day that week I wasn't there.'

Only a twist of fate had saved him, then.

'Rather than seeing myself as a doctor who treated other people, I began to take it more personally. I don't ever want any of my patients to die, but there was one of the victims who was seriously ill and that became a personal challenge. I said: "I am not going to let them take another life." '

I was in a terrorist attack myself, when the IRA hit Canary Wharf. I told the doctor this and remembered that afterwards nowhere felt safe: not work, not the streets, not the train and not even home. There was a sense of violation. 'That's a good word,' he said, this dapper, slender man with his clipped beard and careful sentences, who was badly shaken on the day of the attacks. 'Things you assume are safe are not any more.'

Three bombs were detonated on underground trains on 7 July 2005, each within fifty seconds of each other. As tube stations were evacuated many people tried to catch a bus to work instead. Some of them were on the number 30 moving through Tavistock Square when a fourth bomb ripped it open like a tin can. Fifty-two people died in all that morning, in the four attacks across London. 'The Olympics became inextricably linked in my mind with what happened because I had seen the footage of the announcement that morning,' said Dr Hartle, who found himself unable to look at repeats of that moment even accidentally without breaking down. London was now a mournful, anxious, stressful, dangerous, difficult place to be and work. 'I had to think hard when a colleague invited me to apply to become part of the medical team at the Olympic Games.'

So why say yes? 'Because there was part of me that wanted to be involved in this and make it good, to make up for 7/7. It was really important to me that the Olympics worked, that London could demonstrate that it was about something other than 7/7. That we could deliver something brilliant, to be proud of. We don't do pride very often, and I think we should.' Still, he took a bit of convincing about the actual Olympic Games Making, which asked people to be cheerful and positive and friendly at all times. 'When I sat through the induction training there was lots of waving of hands. I thought: "Oh my God, this will be terrible. I'm going to loathe it."' Then Dr Hartle sat down to watch the opening ceremony put on by Danny Boyle, with its eccentric, inclusive and gloriously inventive vision of our history and what it means to be British, from the smokestack chimneys of the Industrial Revolution to the dancing nurses of the NHS and the surprising sight of Her Majesty the Queen acting alongside Daniel Craig as James Bond, leaving Buckingham Palace in a helicopter, appearing to parachute into the stadium with 007. They timed it brilliantly: I happened to be in the stadium and saw the real Queen come into the stadium with perfect timing, just a few moments after she'd apparently landed, to huge applause.

'I sat on that sofa with tears flowing down my face,' said Dr Hartle, who was watching with his future husband. Early the next morning he travelled to Docklands, where the boxing competition was to be held under his watchful medical eye, and realised things felt very different. 'There was a sense of calm and real excitement. A sense of closure. The Olympics were here. They were cathartic. The anxiety had gone. London was not about 7/7 for me any more.'

A few days later Dr Hartle saw a familiar face as he rode the Central Line towards Docklands in his pink and purple Olympic Games Maker uniform: 'I thought, "It can't be." But it was: Seb Coe. He nodded and smiled then came over and asked what I was going off to do. I told him and he said he was glad we had the right people in the right places. The conversation might have ended there, but I asked him to sign my Olympic Games Maker journal, which made me feel a bit schoolboyish. He thanked me for being part of it, but I said: "No, thank *you*." Then I told him why.'

The doctor was pleased to have been able to say thank you in person but thought nothing more would come of the encounter, until he heard Lord Coe speak about him on the radio. This was towards the end of the Olympic Games and when the boss of it all was asked for a moment that stood out above all others he ignored the brilliance of Mo Farah or Jessica Ennis and chose instead that conversation with Dr Hartle on the underground, which he thought would stay with him for the rest of his life. He quoted the doctor as saying: 'I saw the worst of mankind that morning of the bombs and now I've seen the best.'

The doctor's full name was not given but his phone began to ring anyway. 'Someone texted me to say I was in the *Washington Post*. I thought: "This is bonkers!" I Googled "Andrew Hartle, Olympics" and the first thirty-five pages of results were about this story. It had gone all over the world.' Bad memories and feelings and anxieties were washed away.

'I was incredibly moved by what Seb said,' Andrew told me when we met for the first time, just after the Olympic Games. 'This has drawn a line. I can watch that clip of London being awarded the Olympics and not be pulled back into the past, but feel pride at what we have achieved. Something has ended. This is a new start. We don't often get the chance of that.'

*   *   *

Ten years on, I wonder what good it all did really: what the legacy of the Olympics really was and what it taught us, other than that it's possible for the people of this fractured, troubled, proud country to have a good time, to act with generosity and kindness, to see each other and treat each other as equals. And that's not nothing, is it?

*   *   *

We are all the same under our rags, our finery or our Stella McCartney running gear. Okay, maybe we can't all do what the likes of Sir Mo can do, but even the extraordinarily talented have their flaws. There's a lie going round that you are more worthy of affection if you're famous or rich or have a lot of followers or can run fast. Well, I've met many of those people and I can say that not far below the surface of their pomp, ceremony, fame or notoriety, or the weight of their gold medals, they are just like you and me: anxious, tired, broken, forgetful, impatient; inspiring, engaging, entertaining, sometimes. Human. And we are just like them. We have our own struggles and triumphs, that's why so many of us love sport, because it echoes and amplifies what we all go through, but our stories are worth hearing too. We are worth listening to, whoever we are. I've learned as much in my life from somebody like Andrew or Sharon as I have from somebody famous like Sir Mo.

Or rather Hussein Abdi Kahin, because that's his real name.

The story he told us about himself for years was not true, but the reasons for telling it were heartbreaking. As I write this, the television is showing a clip of him saying: 'For years I just kept blocking out what had happened, but you can only block it out for so long.' The news has just broken. We have just learned that he was not actually reunited with his father here, as we were told so often, because his dad was killed by gunfire in the breakaway state of Somaliland when the boy was just four years old. He came here at the age of eight as a victim of child trafficking, brought to the UK under false pretences by someone who ripped up all evidence of connection with his real family, gave him fake papers and a new name. Some of this reminds me of Sherry, the woman I met at the food bank in North Kensington who had been tricked by her employers and enslaved, although she was an adult and he was just a boy. Hussein, now Mohamed, was made to clean this stranger's house and look after children and act as a domestic servant and not allowed to go to school until the age of twelve, when teachers were told the lie. 'The only thing I could do to get away from this was to get out and run,' he has been saying. As the race wins piled up, the young athlete felt able to confide in his PE teacher and that fine man intervened to save him from his situation. Social services were contacted and told the truth and he was placed with a foster family from Somalia. His life began to improve. The boy was granted British citizenship as Mohamed Farah and given a passport so that he could compete internationally, so he continued to use the name.

'I kept it all locked up,' he has been saying. Now the truth is out the Home Office has promised it will take no action, because children are not responsible for what happens to them; which is a rare case of common sense and justice prevailing. Let's be honest, if he was not famous, if he was not a knight of the realm, if he was not Sir Mo Farah, there is enough evidence to suggest he might not be treated this way.

*   *   *

Islam, Judaism and Christianity all have this idea that we are equal in the sight of God. Young and old, rich and poor, we come into the presence of the divine as equals. God knows, religious institutions have failed to live up to that over the centuries; but the idea is there, as it is in so many other faiths, creeds, paths, traditions and cultures across the world and time, because this is among the best ideas we have had as humans: that everyone is equal and equally loved. Equally lovable. Therefore, we should love each other equally, and when we do, the rules of the world get turned upside down. And briefly, for a while, in the summer of 2012, as the Olympics became the Paralympics, we acted together as if we knew that. It was great. And I remember Mohamed Farah sitting in that Olympic press room after a win, being asked by a reporter if he would not rather be running for Somalia. I remember the intake of breath from those of us who thought we understood what he had been through and the look of hurt on his face for a moment, with a secret backstory none of us knew, before he answered with a wide smile and a deep grace.

'Not at all, mate. This is my country.'

*   *   *

Vera

She sings to me, softly. Not for long, because Nanny's got things to do and she's not the sentimental sort, but there's something about this song she loves and I love her sitting there on the bed, holding my hand, looking into my eyes, which grow sleepy as she sings: 'Up the wooden hills to Bedfordshire, heading for the land of dreams . . .'

I'm under the orange eiderdown in the bedroom at the top of the stairs in her terraced house in Leyton in the early seventies, perhaps 1973, but the song is taking her back to the days before there were grandchildren, before there were children, before her Frank came home from the war, before there was a war. Before the sirens and the shelters and the nights spent watching London burn as a fire warden during the Blitz. Before all that, when life was simpler and sweeter and the brightest light in her life was the way Frank smiled when he came off the football pitch after a win all covered in mud and sweat and joy. Shining. Long ago.

The evening breeze slips in through the open window, bringing the pulse of a reggae bass that unsettles Gladys and brings her back to the moment; and now she's Nanny again and there's washing up to do before Grandad gets back from the pub. So she bends to kiss my cheek and I keep my eyes closed as if asleep and feel the sudden lifting of her weight from the bed and then its absence and hear the creaking of the stairs as she goes down and still the little, fluttering tune turns over and over in my head: '*Up the wooden hills to Bedfordshire . . .*' That's the title as well as the chorus. It's not even a song for kids, really, but sung in the voice of a young woman who is nostalgic for the easier days of child-hood, when big, strong Daddy would lift her onto his shoul-ders and carry her up to bed. They had different tastes in 1936. The singer was not famous then and not even credited on the label, but I wonder if Gladys knew her when it came out. A girl from just down the road with the same name as her sister Vera. One of their own, who had been singing in the local pubs for years. They were both just making their way in the world in the thirties. Neither of them knew what was to come.

*   *   *

And here I am now in a different century, a grown man park-ing a car, trying not to hit a flint wall in a narrow lane in a picture-book village on the South Downs, with seagulls laughing overhead and the same, slight song on my tongue, thinking of Gladys and the last time I saw her, elderly and frail in a care home, holding my hand. I am about to see someone who feels like family because of all of that, but whom I have never met before: Dame Vera Lynn. Someone whose name has become synonymous with courage, defi-ance, resistance, community, endurance and all the values of the wartime generation. Someone who appears in the history books my children bring home from school as one of the faces of the Second World War, alongside Churchill, Hitler and Stalin, but who obviously stands apart from them, not least because she stands for us. The kids know her as the woman of the war, an icon in khaki with a military cap, arms out wide, leading the Blitzed but unbowed people of Britain in a chorus of 'We'll Meet Again', the anthem that will get them through. Dame Vera is someone who was named in a national poll as the woman who most embodied the spirit of the British in the twentieth century. And someone whose dog appears to be eating my boots.

'He likes you,' says the great Dame in a croaky, very elderly voice, but I don't think he does. Digby the Jack Russell is growling and chewing on the toecap of my right boot and I don't want to kick him off for fear of hurting the poor little fella and upsetting his owner, but actually his teeth have pierced the leather and now my toes and it bloody hurts!

'You! No!'

That is the voice of Tom Jones; not the singer, but a former RAF pilot who is married to Dame Vera's daughter Virginia and who is now attempting to take control of the dog. 'It's not a threat,' he declares to Digby, who lets go of my foot but seems unconvinced. Tom tells me the dog was traumatised in the past by a farmer who used to kick him with big boots.

'Shall I take them off?'

'Oh no, I wouldn't do that!'

Digby is taken away, yapping and unhappy, and I rub my toes in the company of a legend. I don't use that word lightly. Not many people deserve it. Dame Vera Lynn, though? Crikey. A legend has built up around her, that's for sure. It's an honour, I say.

'You'll have to speak up,' says her daughter, because Vera is ninety-seven years old now and her hearing is not what it used to be.

'I'm quite deaf, dear,' says Vera with a smile, sitting in an armchair with her hands folded in her lap, wearing a plaid shirt of green, blue and red and a necklace of heavy green beads. The light from a standard lamp behind her illuminates her finely spun white hair and creates a halo. I'm here in the spring of 2013 with Caroline, the wonderful woman from the record company Decca who has made this meeting possible, so that I can write about Dame Vera for the

Telegraph. They are about to put out an album of previously unreleased recordings that will take the Dame back into the charts, the oldest person ever to get there. This is the only interview she will give. Caroline and I are both aware that it may well be her last. 'Probably best not to approach it as an interview, as such,' Caroline has told me, sensitively. 'Maybe think of it more as tea with an elderly aunt.' That's good advice, I realise, as Virginia offers a slice of Victoria sponge and tea in a proper china cup.

*   *   *

Vera was born in East Ham in 1917, the daughter of a docker called Bert and a dressmaker called Annie. As a toddler she had croup and nearly died, but as Vera got older and her lungs recovered it became obvious that the little girl could really sing. In the twenties, before the wireless, that was a precious talent. She earned her first pay for singing in a working men's club at the age of just seven. They paid her seven shillings and sixpence. When Vera left school at fourteen she tried sewing buttons in a factory, but only lasted a day. Nobody was allowed to talk and that didn't suit this gregarious young woman, so her father said: 'Okay, well, you can earn more money in one night of singing than you can in a week at that place.' Her real name was Vera Welch but that surname didn't sound right somehow, so they chose Lynn. Her grandmother's maiden name. It was a family decision.

Vera made her first solo recording in 1936, at the age of eighteen, although she wasn't credited at the time. It wasn't with any of the bands or orchestras she sang with: this was a low-key session with the high, clear purity of her voice backed by nothing more than a murky, mournful organ.

She and Gladys, my grandmother, were the same age, roughly speaking. They grew up in the same place at the same time and were part of that generation of women who lived in the East End but also listened to the wireless, got their news and their music from the airwaves and heard the voices – day after day – of presenters who spoke in the clipped accents of received pronunciation that sound almost comical to us today. Gladys and Vera therefore grew up sounding half Cockney and half like the Queen.

I'm thinking about that when something happens that almost certainly means much more to me than it does to her, but it is truly beautiful. She talks about the song, then starts to sing it, softly: 'Up the wooden hill to Bedfordshire, heading for the land of dreams . . .'

Tears prick my eyes. She sounds just like Nanny used to when she stroked my head. This is Dame Vera Lynn at the age of ninety-seven, singing a song she recorded when she was eighteen years old. Not one of her big hits, it didn't mean a great deal, but it found its way into our family life, into my heart, and she is singing it now, for me. Wow.

✻   ✻   ✻

That was just her opening number. By the time war with Germany was declared in 1939, Vera Lynn was famous as the singer with Ambrose and His Orchestra, a dance band and one of the most popular acts of their day. They toured the country and often appeared on the wireless. 'Radio was the only thing we had,' she says. Somebody asked the soldiers, sailors and airmen preparing to fight which singer they loved the most, and Vera was their choice. After that she became known as the 'Forces' Sweetheart'. The bombs came close very soon. She was singing in a show with the comedian Max Miller at the Holborn Empire in September 1940 when the Blitz began. The Allies had been driven out of France. The RAF had narrowly won the Battle of Britain, but now the Germans chose to send heavy bombers to rain down destruction on cities and civilians. They wanted to break us. They nearly did.

The East End took it hardest first, with 625 tons of high explosive bombs and thousands of incendiaries dropped on the first day, Black Saturday. Gladys and Vera were there, underneath it all. Night after night the bombers kept coming. Nearly six thousand Londoners died in the first month. The docklands and gasworks along the river burned bright as the bombs spread west towards Westminster and Buckingham Palace. Vera continued to sing in the theatre and in nightclubs when she could and to make broadcasts on the radio through all of this. She'd drive from her home in the east to her work in the west in the afternoon, before the raids started, in a little Austin 10 car. 'It had a soft canvas roof,' she tells me. 'That's why I always carried a tin helmet with me. In case the shrapnel came through the roof.'

Vera once told *Desert Island Discs* that if a raid was on the way she would stop the car and get out and lie in the gutter. 'I remember driving one time, it was a horrible wet day,' she tells me now. 'The car skidded and overturned. It landed on its side. People rushed to help me, saying: "Are you all right?" I got out and had a look and I said: "Yes, I'm okay." They righted the car and I said: "Well, I've got to be on my way." I got back in the car but it went de-*doing*-de-*doing* . . . I had broken the axle.'

Still, she kept working anyway, going by bus when she had to.

The whole country seemed to be listening to a radio show of hers called *Sincerely Yours*, which was on air on a Sunday night, directly after the news and often after Mr Churchill. Not just in this country: the programme was aimed at those serving abroad, who sent in thousands of requests for music that would mean something to their loved ones back home. There's an intimacy about the way she talks to them in these broadcasts: 'You'll hear from me again next week. Goodnight, boys.' You can just imagine hearing that in some distant outpost, dreaming of your girl back home or your boy or your mum or whoever it was you longed for. At a time when voices on the radio were so formal and so often full of dreadful news, she sounded warm, close, loving. And all this while bombs were falling. I ask if they kept broadcasting through everything and she says: 'Oh yes. Nothing stopped if there was a raid on.'

Sometimes she sang at the BBC studio in Maida Vale and sometimes from a restaurant in Lower Regent Street called The Hungaria, which declared itself: 'Bomb-proof, splinter-proof, blast-proof, gas-proof and boredom-proof.' Sometimes, if it was impossible to leave, she tried to sleep where she was. 'We used to make ourselves as comfortable as possible on the floor.'

Vera may be ninety-seven but she is mentally sharp and gets cross when she can't remember the number of the bus that used to get her home afterwards. She doesn't think of herself as brave. The song that ended those weekly radio broadcasts was the one that would become her anthem: 'We'll Meet Again'. Vera first heard it at the music publisher's in Denmark Street before the war. 'They had a pianist to play it for the artist, to see if you liked it,' she says. 'They fixed a key for you and did an arrangement. You'd go to the studio and find the band leader there, you'd sing it to them, so he would know how you were going to sing it, when you wanted the music to build up and when to quieten.' Then it was recorded straight away, all live. 'If the trumpeter cracked on the last note you had to do it all over again. You had to do your very best to make sure that the take you did was perfect.'

I tell her about autotune, which means you can now sing off-key and the computer will correct you. She is horrified. 'Keep them in tune? We never sang out of tune! They used to call me One Take Lynn.'

Why does she think 'We'll Meet Again' resonated with so many people? 'It's optimistic,' she says. 'Everyone was separating, going to war. It was a nice lyric. It spoke of hope, you know. We'll meet again. Because you never knew what was happening, from one day to another. A bomb could hit any house, any night.' She remembers a letter that illustrated the danger. 'A man was walking through the streets and he saw a billboard up with me performing somewhere. He thought, "Yes, I know that girl, I listen to her on the radio, I'll go and see her." He stopped and went in and saw me perform. And when he got home, his house had gone. It got a direct hit. So he always said I saved his life.' She laughs then, a deep, hearty laugh of pleasure, at having been able to do some good, somehow, that one time.

'We'll Meet Again' had been written as the world braced itself for war, anticipating a time when mothers and fathers and daughters and sons and husbands and wives and lovers would be separated, as she says, and would long for the day of reunion. A song for the parting, a promise for the future, to be sung or spoken at the railway station, on the quayside, at the crossroads; and an idea to keep them going through the tough times to come, even if they all knew there was a chance that what they were singing about and hoping for might not come true, at least in this life.

*   *   *

'We'll Meet Again' taps into something very old, perhaps as old as life, certainly as old as ancient Rome, where the notion of the afterlife involved being transported to a further place beyond death, where those we love are waiting. For early Christians, informed by the beliefs of Rome, that reunion was a key part of heaven. The Torah promises the Jewish faithful that their loved ones will be there for them when the time comes. The Qur'an says the righteous will see their families again in Jannah, the heavenly realm. The Persian poet Rumi, at least in one modern translation, writes of a field that lies way beyond wrongdoing and right doing, and says: 'I'll meet you there.' Not every religion contains this idea, but many do, and nowhere is it heard more powerfully than in the songs that grew up out of slavery in the American South. Those spirituals say that, against all the odds, things may be bad now, but they will not be bad forever, because life is not meant to be this way, because God is on our side and God is love, and one day everything that is wrong will be made right, there will be no more sorrow, there will be only joy, and those of us who have been torn apart will run into each other's arms again, if not in this life then the next. My friend Mark Halliday, who died from cancer in his forties, far too young, was a fine poet who wrote this as the end approached, seeing what was coming. I reproduce it here with the permission of his family, about and for whom it was written:

'After' by Mark Halliday

I will drift gently upwards until I see
the great golden gates in front of me.
Slowly I'll approach and wait.
'Well done,' the voice will say,
indicating one of many mansions,
mine for millions of days.
But I won't walk in.

I'll quietly ask for five chairs
and I'll sit there beside the gate
and wait, with four to spare.
The first phase of eternity
will be spent watching
for early signs
that you are on your way.
As you arrive, one by one,
you can sit down beside me
while I say,
'Tell me everything that I missed.'
Then I'll listen as the story
of your lives unwinds
like a ball of golden wool –
the day you binned your bike stabilisers,
the day you swam across the pool,
how you spent your birthdays,
the day you left school.
When we are finally all together,
only then will we stand and walk into eternity,
a family of five forever,
tightly gripping each other's hands
like we used to when
we crossed the busy road
to the park.

'We'll Meet Again' also worked powerfully for those who
didn't believe in any kind of afterlife, like my grandmother
Gladys. She didn't believe in God, but she believed in Frank,
and she had to believe she would see him again, literally, in
flesh and blood with big strong arms and kissable lips; it was
what kept her going. She insisted on it, as so many others
insisted on their own truths. We find hope any way we can,

and on a very simple level this song is a song of resistance, on behalf of suffering humans who refuse to give in. You've got to sing something, so why not sing that? You can sing it even if you don't believe in heaven, even if you don't really know what it means, even if you think it's irrational, because on some base level, deep in your gut, the song is a promise that somehow things will be better, somehow everything will be okay, some sunny day.

*   *   *

Vera was as brave as the boys who were listening and she asked to be sent to the front line in the jungles of Burma. 'I was getting letters from the boys and I thought I would like to go and see who I had been singing to.' The trip she took in 1944 was 11,000 miles each way. Was she scared? 'I can't say I really felt scared. I never went anywhere on my own,' she says. 'Not that there was anywhere to go, because I was in the jungle. I was always well looked after by the boys. In the concerts, there were always guards around the perimeter.'

Today's performers would not dream of entertaining the troops without an entourage, a stylist, a make-up artist, a sound system and a security detail. She went to where the fighting was with a pianist and a pistol. 'We stopped in the jungle somewhere along the way and I tried to practise with the pistol. I wasn't very good.' Vera is slipping back in time in her mind as she speaks. 'So I can't say I ever felt scared, although I woke up one morning and there were four Japanese prisoners leaning against my basha, the little grass hut that I was living in. They had been captured in the night. I had to step over their legs to get by them. The look I got. This young girl walking by in little khaki shorts. I shouldn't think they had ever seen a white girl.' Was she worried then? 'No. The boys were around to protect me.' She was at the supply base for the Battle of Kohima, everything having been dropped in by air. How far away was the fighting? 'The battle was up the hill. I was at the bottom of the hill.'

One day Vera stumbled into the wrong tent and found herself in a makeshift operating theatre, where they were trying to save a soldier who had been shot. 'They were digging this bullet out of a boy's arm. I apologised to them for interrupting. The surgeon followed me out and said: "Here's a souvenir." He gave me this bullet on a little piece of lint with all the blood still on it. I had it for donkey's years. I lent it to the Imperial War Museum and I never got it back.' She should get in touch with them, I say, and Vera laughs. 'Yeah. "Where's my bullet?" '

She performed on the back of a truck, and in a cowshed that had been half torn down to make a stage. They used an old-fashioned microphone plugged into the batteries for searchlights. A lipstick was all the glamour she could take. 'I went out with a bag to sling on my shoulders, that was about it. I took a dress but I couldn't wear it because of the mosquitoes. If I went out with my sleeves rolled up the boys would shout at me: "Roll your sleeves down!" ' They didn't mind her having bare legs though, did they? 'No,' she says, and I bet they didn't. 'Make-up was no good, it would run. I didn't have a lady companion or anything. I only had six thousand men.' That was how many she sang to in one day. 'I just washed my hair in a bucket and left it. I'd had a perm before I went, so it was all frizzy.'

She shows me a picture of her being presented with a bouquet of jungle flowers wrapped in surgical gauze. 'One of those boys there didn't get back.'

The photographs show the men looking slightly dazed by the company of this beaming beauty. These are her boys. The legend of Vera Lynn is that she was welcomed like one of them, but in the photograph she shows me, I have to say, there are some men who look at her sideways in a hungry way, like they have more on their mind than a sing-song. Was there really never any trouble? 'Absolutely not. They behaved perfectly. I reminded them of their wives, their girlfriends, their sisters. They treated me with the greatest respect.' She was, it must be said, in the most dangerous and unglamorous of circumstances, absolutely gorgeous. 'Thank you. They behaved like gentlemen.'

Vera was married by then, to Harry Lewis, a member of the RAF band The Squadronaires. She was away in Burma for three months. I'm startled to learn what it was that she did when the war ended. While others were at wild parties, Vera was in a horrifying place. 'The day after peace was declared, I was in Germany entertaining the troops. The government phoned me up and said: "We want you to go." So, I packed up and went.'

Vera sang her stirring, uplifting songs for the soldiers who had only recently liberated the concentration camps. 'They took me round the ovens, where they used to gas people. I saw the gas chambers. They were like a row of garages with steel doors. No birds were flying. They said the gas was still in the air and no birds would fly.'

*   *   *

Vera worked on a pop career after the war and became the first British performer to top the charts in America in 1952. Her last number one in Britain came two years later with 'My Son, My Son'. As it happens she and Harry had a daughter, Virginia, who now manages her mother's affairs. For the next thirty years Vera made radio and television programmes, continued to record albums and toured with particular success in Canada and Australia. She worked hard for charities associated with the war veterans and was made a Dame in 1975, when the Queen said to her: 'You've been waiting a long time for this.'

Way back in wartime, Vera Lynn had sung for the young Princess Elizabeth at her sixteenth birthday party. They had become associated with each other over the years, so it was fitting that her last major public appearance was outside Buckingham Palace, where she led the crowds in a singalong to mark the fiftieth anniversary of the end of the war in Europe. The song, inevitably, was 'We'll Meet Again'. Those celebrations were huge, but they also felt like the end of an era. Dame Vera gave a remarkably strong performance for a woman already pushing eighty, then kissed the boys in Chelsea Pensioner red and headed off into retirement. Harry died four years later, after fifty-eight years of marriage. So many of those who sang along with her have gone.

I ask what music she listens to now for comfort or pleasure and the answer is surprising. 'I don't listen to music.' Why not? 'I don't know. I never have done. The only time I used to listen to it was when we recorded it, to see if it was okay. I don't listen to the radio. I would rather watch television. I'd rather see action.'

She is getting tired. There is one more thing I want to ask, which is sensitive. Vera is ninety-seven years old. Long may she live, but nobody can go on forever. Sacred songs have been part of her repertoire, so what does she think comes next? 'I think there has to be something. What it is, I don't know,' she says. 'I wasn't brought up to pray.' There is a long pause. She is uncomfortable. 'It's a difficult subject.' She may sound a little afraid, but it strikes me that for a singer of sentimental songs, Dame Vera is remarkably unsentimental. She has always faced challenges with a matter-of-fact attitude that defies death or danger. Singing through the Blitz?

Just get on with it, girl. Risking life and limb to get to Burma and cheer up the boys? A matter of duty. And whatever does come next, she will take it as it comes. She may be frail now, but I tell her that for the rest of time she will be the bright-eyed girl with her arms open, singing to the troops.

'Well, that is lovely, really. I didn't set out to be anything like that. I was singing since I was seven. I developed what I had. People used me, in a way, to do something, and I was glad of it. I was just doing my job.' As I'm leaving, she asks a question I find really quite shocking: 'When they write about the war, will they include me in it?'

What she's really asking, in her modest way, is: 'Will they remember me?'

And I say: 'Yes, Vera. I really think they will.'

*   *   *

And now I'm almost crying, because it's the summer of 2020 and the world is in lockdown. None of us can see the ones we love. Some of us are all alone and lonely. Some are mourning those who have been lost and Vera is on the radio again. The Queen has been addressing us from Windsor Castle, finding the right things to say, comparing these dark days to the war and calling us to show the same spirit her generation did, even using words that quote her old ally Vera's song: 'We should take comfort that while we may have more still to endure, better days will return: we will be with our friends again; we will be with our families again; we will meet again.'

A video has been made for the seventy-fifth anniversary of VE Day, which begins with footage of Dame Vera in black and white, shining bright, singing a duet down the ages with Katherine Jenkins. Suddenly it has new meaning. Some day soon, it seems to be saying, we will not have to keep our distance from each other, we will not have to wear masks and stay at home. This version of the song is also sung by soldiers, by nurses, doctors, tube drivers, vets, dentists, pharmacists, road diggers; by people from all walks of life, standing apart for safety, singing together to the camera, trying to keep smiling through. And it's beautiful. Inspiring. It shows the way a song can connect us – even a very old song, which still seems to have so much power. But that's not what is getting to me.

I'm listening to another new recording of 'We'll Meet Again' released during lockdown, this one by the stars of the West End, whose theatres have gone dark in the way they did when the Luftwaffe was overhead. And here among these defiant voices is that of Dame Vera, now aged a hundred and three. The clarity and purity of old is gone. Her voice has been sunk low and laced with gravel by the ravages of age, and she is speaking now instead of singing, but it is still her. And it still reminds me of my nan and the song she used to sing to me at bedtime; and as I write this in the summer of 2020 they are saying on the news that Dame Vera has gone too. She's climbed the wooden hill a final time, the girl they all loved, whose voice was a comfort and who was a light in the darkness. The woman who defied the bombers, who dared to go to the jungle, who wept at the sight of the gas chambers and who kept singing long after the war was over, keeping the memory alive, expressing all the things her people could not say, the last of them still on active service as she was called in her old age; still defiantly insisting, here and now, right to the very end, almost with her last breath, on behalf of us all, in a time of plague, that we will, we surely will, in whatever way we can, however we mean it – and I don't know what it means but it means something – we will meet again, some sunny day.

*   *   *

Ronnie and Reggie

I owe my working life to the most vicious men in Britain, as they were known then. Ronnie and Reggie Kray, gangster brothers once photographed in sharp suits and skinny ties by David Bailey as the Swinging Sixties happened around them, despite them. He made a famous monochrome image of their mean and moody faces: Ronnie with his hooded eyes and slicked-back, oil-black hair; Reggie standing at an angle behind him in a contrasting grey suit, a looming presence with a quizzical look.

If Ronnie was mad, as the doctors would later certify, they were both bad and dangerous to know. The twins were born within ten minutes of each other in 1933, just down the road from where my grandmother Gladys and Vera Lynn were both making their way in the world and three years before Vera's first recording. I daresay their mother Violet sang a tender verse or two of 'Up the Wooden Hills to Bedfordshire' when she put them to bed. These East End boys grew into West End nightclub owners, who relished ordering drinks to be poured for the likes of Judy Garland and Frank Sinatra. They also ran a gang called The Firm that went in for armed robbery and protection rackets, hurting people who crossed them and creating connection through fear: 'Do as you're told, pay up and nobody gets hurt. The place doesn't get burned down. Now isn't that better? Ain't we pals?'

Ronnie wrote an autobiography, because they really were that famous, and he said: 'Me and my brother ruled London. We were untouchable.'

Except they weren't. The police came for them at dawn one day in May 1968, while the boys were lying with a couple of young women in the beds they kept at their parents' flat in Bethnal Green. Mum and Dad were away on holiday in Suffolk at the time.

The Krays were sent down for murder, but their legend lived on in the East End. And it really was a legend, full of lies, exaggerations and delusions about these post-war folk heroes who had dared to muscle their way in on Establishment territory Up West. We knew all about them when I was growing up. Their people still ran crime in our area, to a degree, even in the early eighties. The drug runners and gun gangs from other nations were muscling in, but the name of the Krays was still feared, for the moment. They never hurt their own – that was what people said. Except, of course, for Jack the Hat McVitie, who was stabbed multiple times in the head and body by a frenzied Reggie. Or wild-haired Frank Mitchell, the Mad Axeman, who was sprung from prison because they thought he would be useful but who turned out to be too strong, too unstable and too unmanageable. Frank was shot in the back of a van, then taken out to sea and his body dumped overboard. Then there were those they saw as rivals, like George Cornell, a member of the Richardson gang, shot by Ronnie at the Blind Beggar pub in the Whitechapel Road.

They loved their mum though. That was part of the legend and it was definitely true. Ronnie and Reggie loved Violet Kray obsessively and she loved them just as much in return, having brought them up single-handedly while their dad Charlie was on the run from the Army. 'My lovely boys', she called them. Ronnie was in prison when Vi died in August 1982, so he had time to write a poem that went like this:

Mum you are like a rose.
When God picked you,
You were the best Mum he could have chose.

You kept us warm when it was cold,
With your arms around us you did fold.
For us, you sold your rings of gold.

When you died,
I like a baby cried.
When I think of you,
it is with pride;
So go to sleep Mum,
I know that you are tired.

That's not the greatest poem in the world, but it is poignant from a man who was approaching his fiftieth birthday inside Parkhurst Prison and who must have known he would never get out. However, the twins were allowed to snatch a breath of fresh air by attending Violet's funeral at Chingford Old Church, up the posh end of the East End, making their first appearance in public since their arrest thirteen years earlier. There was a thrill in the air. And this is where I come in, aged fifteen and scared of everything and everybody.

I remember listening to the radio in my bedroom late at night, when an unknown singer from Barking called Billy Bragg appeared on John Peel's Radio 1 show, singing in our accent and covering a song called 'Fear is a Man's Best Friend'. The Krays knew the truth of that. I was about to find out for myself that fear can change your life.

* * *

I went to a terrible school. Sir George Monoux is great now, apparently, but in the summer of 1982 it was a failing comprehensive and a bit of a war zone. Fighting in the playground, fighting in the classrooms, fighting among the teachers, although their conflict was mostly in words, not kicks and punches like ours. Old Mr Grimface would prowl up and down the hall in his batwing gown while we did detention, each of us standing and facing the front. For an hour. In stifling, indoor heat. If you moved, you had to come back another day. If you trembled and wobbled and fainted with potential heat stroke, you were left there. If you complained, you were told to report to his office the next day, to face the Angel of Death. Grimface would order you to stand still, then climb onto his own desk with his cane, grip it with both hands and jump, swooping down to slash at your palms. He had been in the war, of course. He could have worked for the Krays. He was led away from school one celebrated day foaming at the mouth after a meltdown in the classroom. My mum felt sorry for him, but she had never suffered the Angel.

Meanwhile, long-haired Mr Young-Buck was 'teaching' us sociology in his skinny jeans, doing nothing to stop the chaos while his eyes followed Miss Magnifique the French teacher out in the corridor. To be fair, it was a boys' school and most of our eyes were following her too. Not much education was going on. If you were different, you got hit. I don't mean different because of your skin colour though, that didn't seem to matter most of the time. We were all kinds of colours and the boys who carved NF for National Front on their desk were seen as weirdos. No, it was dangerous to be different in other ways. Gay, for example. That would get you a proper beating. Reading a book in public was good for a punch. Paying attention in class or any kind of swotting, like answering a question without a sneer on your face? Bosh. The way to behave was to act bored at all times, even if you weren't. And I really wasn't, when the editor of the local newspaper came to visit.

His name was John. This rakish figure in sideburns and seventies flares looked desperately out of fashion to a room full of cocky-insecure two-tone rude boys in drainpipe trousers, but he dared to talk to us anyway and something he said cut through the ennui and ignorance and hit home with me: 'If you become a journalist, you could have a great life. Look at Michael Parkinson.' The obvious reply to that would have been to ask why he was stuck there with us, rather than hobnobbing with the rich and famous, but nobody could be bothered. I didn't realise at the time that the editor was on a relatively low wage, working long hours, giving his all to the job. All I heard in that moment was the name of a man we called Parky, who hosted the most popular talk show on television. He had just interviewed Muhammad Ali, by far the most exciting man I had ever seen in my life. The heavyweight champion of the world, the motormouth, the gorgeous, beautiful, defiant, elegant, irresistible showman who took no shit from nobody and was an undeniable hero. I wanted to be Ali. This was not a viable career path for several reasons, including a reluctance to be hit; so I figured that being Michael Parkinson might be the next best thing.

The editor of the *Walthamstow Guardian* said Parky had begun on the *South Yorkshire Times*, which showed local papers were the starting point for a career that could take you to the stars. 'Would anyone like to see for yourself, on work experience?'

Not a hand went up. He looked confused and hurt, not realising what was at stake if we expressed any kind of interest at all. Far safer not to. But afterwards, when every-one else had rushed out to play football, I dared to approach him.

'Can I do it? You know, come?'

'Sure. Great. Pop in the office, ask for Sandra. She'll sort you out.'

He smiled, this man who was offering me a way out I desperately wanted. A careers adviser had only just asked me what I wanted to be after school. I couldn't tell him the truth – David Bowie was already David Bowie, there was no vacancy – but I had found an edition of *Penguin Modern Poets* somewhere and the barfly voice of Charles Bukowski appealed to me, so I said: 'I want to be a writer.' I'm not saying the career adviser laughed, although he certainly smirked. We were allowed to imagine ourselves as rock stars or football players, but the world of literature was way out of bounds to boys like me, in his view. I imagine him sighing at the death of his own university dreams, twiddling a pencil and glancing at the clock to see if it was time for a liquid lunch and a fag yet. 'What do you want to do though, seri-ously? You're a bright lad, how about a job in a bank?'

Sticking two fingers up at him was a big part of the reason I dared to enter the offices of the *Walthamstow Guardian* in Fulbourne Road, Walthamstow, in August 1982, for work experience at the age of fifteen. The newsroom was noisy with the bang and clatter of thirty or so typewriters, because in those days local papers had staff and there were three different titles sharing the same space. The air was blue with the smoke of cigarettes sucked in thought or burning in ashtrays while fingers flew. I was overwhelmed, bewildered and intimidated by the most adult gathering I had ever been in, particularly as I approached the obvious leader of the pack, the chief reporter, an Irishman called Alan whose eyes seemed to ask: 'Who are you then and what have you got to offer?'

The answer was nobody and nothing; but those eyes also sparkled with mischief and welcome. He was a gifted reporter who could charm a story out of anyone. Alan suspected I was only there because the editor wanted to curry favour with my dad, who was a local Labour councillor, but in time he would turn out to be a generous, supportive teacher and a big influence on my journalistic life, at least in the early days. At that moment, though, it seemed like all the scary, dark, unknown secrets of the adult world were bound up in him. I was frightened of him. That's important to this story. I was more frightened of the chief reporter than I was of the Krays . . . until I came face to face with the twins and their people.

*   *   *

The funeral happened three days into my work experience. It was a really big deal. Violet was carried in a flower-laden hearse all the way up from Bethnal Green to the church on the hill in Chingford, a distance of ten miles. Out of the busy city to the suburbs, away from the noise and pollution to a peaceful place surrounded by trees and relative prosperity. A journey taken by so many East End families over the decades, including my own. I've seen reports that suggest 60,000 people turned out to see her go past. But why? It was a hot day, the schools were on holiday and this was a free spectacle, the closest thing we had to a royal parade. We were more used to acting collectively in those days than we are now, at street parties and carnivals and because there was still a sense of connection to each other through the lingering idea of the old East End. The otherness created in the days of death and destruction, when our grandparents stood together to resist the Nazis, or so we were often told. Churchill had used the Cockney resilience to tell the rest of the country to buck up their ideas, because if the East End could take a battering and still survive with a smile, surely Bristol or Manchester or Glasgow or Belfast could do the same? The sentimental soundtrack to this story was the music of Vera Lynn and we know how brave she and other women like her were during this time, as hellfire rained down. There really was courage and endurance and community in the East End during the Blitz and a determination to survive together that was really extraordinary. But there was also another side to it all, which emerged decades later through the work of the historian Angus Calder. Crime soared under the bombardment, bad things happened in the blackout, houses and bodies were looted far more frequently than my grandparents would have let on.

They were defiant though, and not just to Hitler. Churchill was booed when he visited West Ham in 1945, which shook him and gave an early clue to the Labour landslide to come; and it was because people didn't want things to go back to the way they had been before the war, which was all the prime minister was promising. That would have meant days of champagne and plenty for the likes of him, but a return to depression and poverty for them. They wanted a better life and having fought for it they were prepared to vote or use any other means necessary to get it. The rise of a powerful pair of East End boys like the Krays who refused to kowtow to the Establishment or the law was almost inspirational to some. They were robbing hoods rather than Robin Hoods, but Ronnie and Reggie somehow became symbols of that mythical time before when things had been better: when neighbours knew each other's names, doors were left open and children could play safely in the street (except the pretty young lads who had to run when Ronnie came by, but strike a light, the older generation in Cockney Dreamland didn't want to talk about that). They were stars, for sure. Still powerful to some, fascinating to others, even if only as caged survivors of a bygone age, let out for the first time since the Beatles split up.

Alan weaved through the crowds to the churchyard and I did my best to keep up. When we got there, he surprised me by suggesting I should tag on to the end of the line of mourners and try to get in to the church.

'Sorry?'

'Go on, you don't look like a reporter.'

This was true. I was wearing a black tie and a black jacket like a lot of the journalists, but I was also fifteen years old. Yes, he was apparently asking a child to gatecrash the funeral of the mother of the two most notorious men in Britain. No, I didn't realise how dangerous it was, but I wasn't stupid: I had no intention of doing anything of the sort. I slipped into the crowd and out of his sight, so I could walk around a bit then come back and say it hadn't been possible, but something unexpected happened.

The crowd parted, like the Red Sea before Moses.

They saw the jacket. They saw the black tie. They saw my age and must have thought I was related to the Krays. Nobody wanted to get in the way of a relative of those two, so suddenly I found myself next to other mourners in black. Ahead of us I could see two of the biggest guards the prison service had been able to find, and between them, only just visible, the head of Ronnie Kray bobbing in the line, his black hair still slicked back like it was in their heyday. Reggie must have been there somewhere too. Slowly, the mourners moved inside the church. I could feel myself getting closer to the entrance and started to panic, but I didn't know what to do. If I ran I would give the game away. If I stayed I was in danger of being beaten up. I knew that now.

The church porch loomed over me. I could see the dark interior through the doorway and smell the musk of wood and history, but a huge man was also there. A bouncer or a security guard or a policeman, I don't know, but he was massive, blocking out the light in a black suit with his eyes hidden behind shades. He took one step forward to stop me going any further, looked down with his arms crossed and said in a quiet, discreet but intensely threatening voice: 'You. Must. Be. Fucking. Joking.'

I ran then. I ran and ran through the crowds, running for my life.

I ran all the way back to Alan, who was laughing his head off. I don't think he had really meant me to try and enter the church. I think he had been joking, because that was the newsroom culture in those days: the next workie after me was given a number and told to ring a Mr Albert Hall for a quote, but found herself talking to the box office. In any case, word got back to the editor, who called me in to his office with a smile on his face and said something like: 'Listen, son, if you're willing to gatecrash the funeral of Violet Kray for a story then you can have a job with us, as soon as you're old enough!' I joined the paper as an apprentice the following summer, having only just turned sixteen. Maybe he thought I was fearless, I don't know. In truth it had all been an accident. I never had the nerve to tell him.

* * *

Joining the local paper was my big break, a way to break the class ceiling and get away, so I quit school and went for the training instead. Years and years later, having somehow made the nationals, I went to interview the original inspiration for all this, Michael Parkinson. That was a thrill. It was early in the morning, too early for my liking, at a pub run by his son in the Berkshire countryside. Parky was in an armchair when I entered, wrapped up against the cold in a Crombie coat and scarf, looking older and paler than he had once done on the television, but a lot of time had passed since he sparred with Ali. He stood up quickly though and crossed the floor of the pub to meet me halfway, making direct eye contact, smiling warmly and pumping my hand before saying, unprompted: '*Walthamstow Guardian*? I'm *South Yorkshire Times*. We are two of a kind.'

What a lovely thing to do. I was nearly overcome with emotion, right there and then. What a pro, too. The sly old fox had done his research and established his place in the hierarchy, therefore gaining an advantage in the interview to come. I still managed to get a good news line out of him though, as my own little tribute. We talked about a car crash of an interview he had recorded with Helen Mirren in the seventies, which had come up on social media more recently when she remembered it as a particularly sexist encounter.

'I'm not a sexist,' said Parky with conviction. 'I'm Yorkshire.'

That made a few headlines. He got publicity for his book. And, actually, the thing I learned most from Michael Parkinson about interviewing is that it should never be a contest, never adversarial like the one with Helen Mirren, not if you want to put people at ease to really find out what they think, which is when things get interesting.

The most important thing is to listen. I know it sounds obvious, but it is surprising how many people don't listen carefully enough to what the other person is saying, whether that's as a reporter, a boss interviewing someone for a job, a renter looking for a new flatmate, a parent trying to raise kids, someone out on a hot date or just a friend having a chat. Most of what I'm about to say applies in all those situations and more.

I have learned not to just ask a question and sit there fretting about what the next one will be, as I used to when I was younger, but to listen closely. If they go off on a tangent I follow for a while, because it might lead somewhere interesting. I'm not afraid to ask what might sound like a stupid question but I do like to make sure I know what they're talking about. I research like a demon in the days before an interview, make copious notes but leave them all at home. I memorise everything I can instead of taking the notes with me and have their life, work, achievements, failures, joys and heartbreaks in my head, so that I am able to recognise it when they say something that really matters to them. The alternative to this if you're not a journalist or don't have time to prepare so manically is to be curious, really curious, pay close attention and be unafraid to ask what they mean if you hear anything unexpected or out of character. I once interviewed Paul Michael Glaser, the actor who was Starsky in the American cop show *Starsky & Hutch*, when he came to England to play Captain Hook. I thought the most interesting thing about him was the way he had processed the tragedy of losing his wife and daughter to AIDS-related illness, after blood transfusion. I wasn't allowed to ask about that, however. My questions had to be strictly about pantomime, which was not promising given that he was an American who had never been in one before and clearly didn't know anything about the tradition. Why should he?

The interview went as well as expected, which is to say badly. The chat was dull and disjointed. The press officer for the small town theatre was standing at the door of the dressing room about to end the misery for both of us by calling time when Mr Glaser, out of boredom or for the want of anything else to say, muttered: 'Anyway, it's all just a distraction from the fear of death.' I knew, because I had done a deep dive into his life, that this was highly significant to him, privately. He was referring to a way of seeing the world that had helped him after Elizabeth's death. The phrase had caught my eye in a speech he once gave to a business school, which I had found buried deep in his website, so I mentioned it. 'You said that in a speech at Harvard, didn't you?'

He looked at me directly for the first time, realising I had made a connection.

'Could you tell me a little bit more about what you meant?'

Paul Michael Glaser thought for a moment then looked over to the press officer, told her politely that he would finish when he was ready and spent the next hour or so talking in a quite beautiful and moving way about all he and his wife had been through. There was space between us for that to happen because I had done my research and known what he meant when he was muttering to himself. I had listened and picked him up on the cue and taken him seriously. An interview should feel more like a collaboration than a fight (unless a fight is what they want, in which case I may well give them one. Certain politicians come to mind). Most of the time the people I meet have got things they feel they need to say, perhaps about their latest project. I want them to feel heard and once they have got all that off their chest I can ask the questions I need to in order to please my editor; but I hope it doesn't stop there. I hope the time we have shared and any connection that has built up between us will open up the chance for something unexpected to happen. When they have done their duty by speaking about X and I have done mine by asking about Y, when we're just two people talking about whatever comes to mind, that's when Z can come up.

Or A or B, F or P, who knows? The surprising, the challenging, the moving and the beautiful all have the chance to pop up in the conversation now and they're very welcome.

There may also be something deep inside that a person is dying to say, whether they know it or not, even if their partner, publicist or manager or their own more cautious self has decided it should not be said. Truthfulness can sit in the chest like trapped wind. Sometimes my job is to put a metaphorical arm around that person and burp them like a baby, although sometimes whatever it is pops out of their mouth anyway. This can happen in even the most difficult and challenging of circumstances, as in the Tiger Woods story I tell elsewhere in this book. To get there, be attentive. Work out what the other person wants and try to help them with that. Go with the flow. Watch the body language. Put your friendly face on. Don't be afraid, you may find they want conversation and connection. This encounter can work for both of you. Maybe they're lonely. Maybe they're flattered. Maybe they are not sure about the direction they're going in and are absolutely thrilled to have met someone friendly and pleasant who shows signs of knowing who they really are, what they stand for and what they should be doing. I have seen very famous people melt for all those reasons and heard at least one of them say she felt understood for the first time in her life. She was surrounded by sycophants and hangers-on and managers who wanted to exploit her and had been pursued by predatory men all her life, so perhaps it was no surprise that a little empathy went such a long way.

There is one thing I have had to learn the hard way though, and it is that when you are talking to somebody very famous it is never about you. If they bond with you, it's possibly just because they need a friend that day. That's true even if you end up going for a drink, racing down country lanes in a vintage Ferrari and going on a pub crawl long into the night, until they invite you to stay at their house, as once happened with me and a former celebrity bad boy who had been behaving himself lately in order to keep his job but who wanted to let his hair down just a little that day and needed company. Expect to be dropped when they've finished with you. Don't feel hurt, it's nothing personal, some people just see others as servants. Not just the rich and famous ones either, in my experience. But those are the exceptions, because I find most people are happily respectful.

What if you're not a journalist but interviewing someone for a job or even meeting them for the first time on a date? I'd say the same is true: listen, above all else. Make eye contact. Be yourself. Be interested. Think about what the other person wants and needs in the moment. Work out what matters to them. Who are their friends and colleagues? Who do they care about? Have patience, compassion, empathy. Look for wisdom. Be present, in the moment. Keep that eye contact going. Don't look away. Don't check your phone, for goodness' sake. What do you think you're doing? How would you like it if they did that to you? Don't scan the room for someone better to talk to, that's really rude. Don't allow yourself to daydream about what you're having for dinner. Even worse, don't think of them naked, whatever the experts say. Just don't. Seriously. Look at them properly. See what they're wearing, how they sit, how they stand, when they feel the urge to clear their throat, what they do with their hair. Do they fiddle with a ring, for example? Helen Mirren played Elizabeth in the movie *The Queen* as a disciplined, highly self-controlled woman who twisted her wedding ring repeatedly at stressful moments, a tiny sign of the tension she was not allowed to show but which had to come out somewhere. Look for signs like that. They are what psychologists, magicians and hustlers call tells. They give a lot away. Remember their name. Let them know you do know a little something about what they are talking about, but don't pretend you know everything. Let them tell their story. Don't jump in on their words or – worse – say that happened to you too and go off on a story of your own. Don't match suffering with suffering, particularly when they don't match.

'I've got a brain tumour.'

'Oh, I've got a headache myself this morning, it was a big night.'

Do let the other person know about any shared experiences, but only if it's right, sensitive and doesn't take the attention from them for too long. Don't try to cover up for not listening by saying something inane like 'cool' or 'great' or 'interesting' because that's really obvious. Do respond to what they are saying with your eyes and your body. Smile, nod, say yes, murmur approval. Ask open-ended questions that allow the other person to reflect but that also mean they have to respond. Say thank you, be encouraging, positive, uplifting; help where you can, even if you profoundly disagree with what they're saying. Play a long game if you need to.

I once interviewed a far-right politician whose views appalled me. I said nothing in our conversation that compromised my own beliefs, but my air of being interested allowed him to relax and make jokes and say things he would not have said, which revealed his true nature for all to see. To put it in the only language he would understand, I gave him enough rope to hang himself. His career ended after that interview was published. It's a brutal example, but the point is that careful attention achieved more than confrontation would have done.

Lorraine Kelly, who hosts a daily talk show on television, has an easy charm and gentle manner that means she is sometimes underestimated by the politicians who appear as guests, but she gets them so relaxed they admit to things they would never normally dare speak of in public. Careers have ended there, too. Lorraine trained on local newspapers like me and Parky. She made her name as a brilliant television reporter in Scotland during the Lockerbie, Piper Alpha and Dunblane disasters because she had a way of making people feel at ease and helping them to tell their stories on camera, even through tears. The next story I want to tell is an encounter with Clive James, who was a journalistic hero to both myself and Lorraine when we were starting out in the eighties, but before we get there I'd like to offer something she shared with me when I interviewed her the other day, which applies whether you are a reporter, a recruiter or just trying to be a decent, friendly human. 'I don't shy away from asking difficult questions, I really don't, but as my granny says: "You can get more with honey than with vinegar."'

*   *   *

Clive

Clive James is dying. He has announced this to the world by writing a poem about a Japanese maple tree which has been bought by his daughter for the garden. His duty now, the poem says, is to live to see the leaves turn to flame. 'That will end the game,' he writes, meaning he won't survive the season, which is the autumn of 2014. I read his words in the paper and I'm sad to think of his fate, but glad to see that a man whose writing I adored as a teenager – and who I once saw as a hero for defying all the class rules that bound us both – is refusing to go gentle into that good night. Leukaemia has done for him, but he will go out in a blaze of glory from the tree, as he says: 'Filling the double doors to feed my eyes, a final flood of colours will live on as my mind dies.'

*   *   *

Clive James is still dying, two years later; but he's opening the door of his surprisingly small Victorian terraced house in a quiet street in Cambridge and welcoming me in and saying, rather sheepishly, that the tree died first. 'We had it replaced,' he says in a weakened, croaky version of that assertive, nasal Aussie voice that was so familiar to so many of us in his days as a television star, when his audiences numbered millions. 'Am I embarrassed to still be here? Yes, highly!' And he chuckles, wheezily.

Clive James is a slighter version of himself today in black shoes, black trousers and a black turtleneck, with wisps of white hair like smoke around a coin-shaped wound on his forehead, the evidence of a recent operation. Back in the day he was the king of prime-time, a bald-headed bulldog in a suit with a face caught between a smile and a scowl, bringing us witty reports from far-flung places and wry documentaries on the power of fame or the weirdness of television: the man with the golden tongue and a supermodel on each arm, full of charm and sometimes smarm but always funny, always sharp, always sort of true. He created his own legend, then told us it wasn't to be trusted, in a memoir called *Unreliable Memoirs,* which burned with veracity and sold like hot cakes. I carried it around one teenage summer like a manual for life, because here was a boy from nowhere, just like me, who reached up and took the gift of words from the tree and ate the apple and got to say what the hell he liked, with eloquence and charm and bite; and they let him in to Cambridge, to the BBC, to all the places boys like us could never be, and all those living rooms through all those TVs, by sheer force of personality. He seduced us all. Here was a man with a brilliant mind who understood our culture and how it was changing before our eyes, who analysed the frivolous as if it were high-toned and told us who we were. And made us laugh. There was a lot of laughter.

If he was before your time, can I just say that was a colossus during the eighties and nineties. You really couldn't escape him. From mad television shows to chat and books of essays, a handful of novels and collections of poetry, for which he has only lately been given the credit he always felt he deserved. Almost too late.

'I feel like I've had a whole other career since I got sick,' he says. 'My problem as a poet before was that people thought I could not be serious; I was a TV face. But when you're on the point of death you look pretty much as serious as you can get.' He coughs, nastily. 'Sorry I'm not just doing this for drama.'

We're in the back room of his simply but elegantly furnished house, which has been adapted for this last season of his life. Sunshine spills through the skylights in the conservatory, a long space that serves as his kitchen, his living room and his library. Clive James lives here alone. He split up with his wife a few years ago, when an alleged mistress turned up from Australia and confronted him on camera in the street. He's made it a rule never to talk about his family or his love life except in print under his own control, but Clive is going to break that today, because what is there left now but words and stories and a desire to say what mattered and what matters? But we start with a book he's pushing, because that's only polite: *Play All* talks about *Game of Thrones* and other box sets he has watched with his daughter of late and argues, convincingly, that long-form television is the art form of our age. 'This reservoir of intelligible drama is unprecedented in history.'

The thing is Clive, I'm thinking, if I was dying, if I had as little time left as you, would I really be watching television? 'The question answers itself. My immediate answer would be no, of course not. It's time to read Boswell's *Life of Johnson* again. But I've done that, and I've found myself watching television. Also, I've got a sense of theatre enough to know it would be interesting to anyone who heard about it that I was sitting there watching television on the point of death. So, I was being mischievous, writing this book.'

Mischievous to the point of perversity, I might say.

'That's okay. That plays. It brought you here.'

And so it did. How is his health right now?

'It could be worse. It's pretty bad. A combination of things including emphysema, but leukaemia is the one that's hard to argue with.'

When he published that poem in 2014 and was gratified to read a tsunami of tributes, Clive James really did think he was about to go; but then the doctors tried a new medicine which had results that surprised everyone, including them. I-brutin-ib. 'Great name for a drug, isn't it? A testosterone name. Sounds like an Arnold Schwarzenegger character from the post-Conan phase.' He coughs again, from deep within. 'I thought I was a goner two weekends ago when I woke up at four thirty in the morning with a tongue bigger than my mouth. It was scary that morning. You can't believe you can breathe because you can't swallow. I was nine hours at Addenbrooke's Hospital getting antihistamines pumped into me through a vein, until it went down.' The doctors don't know if this was because of the leukaemia or the drug. 'I am faced with the prospect that the thing that is keeping me alive is trying to kill me.'

There's no way out now, anyway.

'These drugs won't cure the thing, but they stave it off. I used to have a ton of energy, but now I've got a fraction of it and that won't alter. I'm not going to get well again, but I might get some more time. My legs are very weary. They're heavy and I can't walk far. So I'm that unwell . . . but on the other hand, I'm that well. I'm here, I'm talking to you. My brain is apparently working quite well. I do feel very lucky I've been able to have this extra time to think and to sum up. I feel lucky I've had a life. And I didn't really have to struggle hard with the choice when I was told my various diagnoses. The choice was: do you just lie down and wait for it or do you go on? I just went on quite naturally.'

That is the choice: do we surrender to the end or do we keep going? Rage against the dying of the light, or at least keep breathing, keep wondering, keep reaching out for connection with those around us, looking for a hand to hold as we go, keep writing. 'Paradoxically, I seem to produce quite a lot now, and the reason is very simple: I've got nothing else to do. I can't get out of the house.'

Is that literally true? 'I've been out of the house maybe once or twice this winter, which is over now I suppose.' Indeed, it is nearly summer. 'Not counting my visits to hospital which are constant, but then I just step into the cab to go. My point is, I've got no other plans to make. And I know how to conserve what energy I've got left.'

*　　*　　*

Clive was born in Kogarah, a suburb of Sydney, in 1939. His father survived a Japanese prisoner-of-war camp, but then died in a plane crash on the way home. 'I was born in chaos. The circumstances of my father not coming back from the war shaped my life. People ask me about it as if it was a thing that happened then and I overcame it and moved on, but I never overcame it. That's what I am still doing, overcoming it.'

He was originally called Vivian, after a male tennis player, but hated it. 'I told my mother: "Look, I'm extremely unhappy being called Vivian, could we change it?" She agreed to that. My mother had an extremely bad habit of doing what I wanted. That ruined me and it created me, because it got me used to getting what I wanted.'

He found his new name at the pictures.

'I saw a movie with Tyrone Power playing a character called Clive and I chose that. I must have been ten years old.' Is there any part of him that still feels like Vivian? 'Yes, all the time. Things grow complex and stay with you. I don't think you solve them.'

He knows I'm recording this, there are two machines on the table, but he says: 'My great mistress who was in my life for more than twenty years never used my first name because other people had.' So, what, she gave him a different name? 'She just avoided names. She was amazing. She's still . . . somewhere.'

They're all still somewhere, I say.

'No, some of them are dead,' he says sharply. 'I've been around longer than you. Two or three of my first girlfriends are dead.'

Clive moved to England as a young man and his bright mind got him in to Cambridge to read English. Then he went off like a rocket, becoming president of the Footlights and captaining Pembroke College on *University Challenge*. By the seventies he was a journalist: one of those characters who emerged at that time as champions of the idea that you could come from what he calls 'ordinary circumstances' and still expect to get a great education and make a name for yourself. Charlie Brooker, the creator of *Black Mirror*, is among the many who have called him an inspiration for that. I tell him I agree, mainly because of the memoir.

'You realise how lovely this is to hear? I promise that when you get to this stage, you just want to be useful. I got a letter from a lady who had brought up two kids in very challenging circumstances who said: "Reading you gave me the courage to go to the Open University." Those are unbeatable letters to get. And it's unbeatable to hear what you just said. I mustn't dwell on it because praise and success have always been bad for my personality.'

I can't help feeling he doesn't really mind.

'I have to say it is a bit easier coming from Australia, because there is no class system. The system here is pretty hard to beat, for the British.'

As a critic, he was the first to write about television as a serious work of art. Then he became a very popular presenter himself, with shows collecting the best and worst of TV around the world, most notably the gruelling Japanese game show *Endurance*, which seemed outlandish and cruel at the time but inspired so many of the reality shows we watch today. If you want to know why celebrities are forced to eat kangaroo dicks in the jungle, there's your answer.

And talking of circles of hell, a few years ago he published a translation of Dante's *Divine Comedy*. That was bold. His wife Prue is a world expert on the subject. It was taken as a gesture of love towards her as well as Dante, coming not long after she kicked him out. 'I used to impress my wife by writing poems when we were kids in Australia and she has never forgotten it, God bless her.'

I remember that he fell in love with the *Divine Comedy* as she read it to him in a café in Florence in the sixties. 'When I first knew her she was the most beautiful girl in Australia. In the world. A long time has gone by now and she still is,' he says, tenderly but with regret. 'Things got bad because I wanted to feel that way about every other beautiful girl in the world. But no matter how bad things got, we have all this to share and can't do without each other in that way.'

He looks around the room.

'Books, music, sculpture. It pleases me greatly that she's a great scholar. I find that an endlessly renewable source of interest and love.'

And yet they no longer live together.

'I've made every possible mistake. I'm still here, still married, which is quite incredible, considering my weaknesses. You won't find me going too far with that theme, but you say what you like, you're a free man.'

I've read the poems, I say. They're full of passion.

And he says, quickly: 'Don't forget, the Dante was for her.'

*   *   *

And now the picture editor has arrived. She is called Stephanie and she would like him to sit on a throne to have his portrait taken, because he has written about *Game of Thrones*. But Clive says: 'No, not a throne. I don't like to do tricks. You may have to take that away. I have no ambitions to sit on a throne, contrary to some people's belief.'

Still, he is very taken by Stephanie, who is French and has an accent he likes. 'I could keep you talking forever,' he says and is gratified when she laughs and appears pleased. 'Stick around. I'm a tremendous flirt in all languages.' When she's gone to tell her team not to bring in the throne, he sighs. 'She doesn't know it, but she's got a smile that could start a war.'

Clive drags out the last word, enjoying it to the full, then mutters: 'I broke my heart a million times. They're all on the same fault line, the same scar.' I worry that he's tiring and say I don't want to keep him too long. 'No, please do.' And he mutters again, this time words he thinks I might write: ' "Clive James talking too long about the implications of the mere existence of Stephanie." '

There is no doubt he thinks of himself as a romantic.

'The Italians used to call it the *visione amorosa*. It's a divine vision, the vision of love. It's a thing in itself. Different human beings walk in and occupy that space and over and over again you are faced with this blow to the heart of what you hope to attain but cannot have. It explains everything. It explains the Trojan War.'

It goes on hammering at his heart, even as the rest of his body fails. 'Even now, there's a girl I meet every three weeks in the immunoglobulin infusion unit and I would fight my way through a lake of crocodiles just to get a glimpse of her. The mere suggestion of what might happen is enough.'

I wonder how he deals with all this longing, stuck in this room, and he gestures towards the books. 'I write those.

Libido doesn't vanish entirely, because there are mental patterns associated with it that aren't going to go away, but I deal with the longing mainly as I've always dealt with it, as a writer.' So there's a connection with his creativity? 'I can't be hypocritical on this subject. I have to say that falling in love, a thing that happened often, could happen in five minutes. It could happen now as I walk – no, shuffle – down the street. It could happen. I regarded that as a direct injection of energy into my creative impulse. And it was – and still would be if I was out there.' He looks down the long room towards the door to the street. 'I've had this conversation with several men in my life – writers like us – and I'm sure they all suffer from what we suffer, but some of them are very good at hiding it.'

He says this as if I am part of his circle of writers now and I am, of course, ridiculously flattered. I know what the old seducer is doing, but I'm still falling for it. Does he have any regrets? 'I've got almost nothing but regrets. Things I shouldn't have done and things I should have done better. But I'm lucky that I'm inherently a merry man, even though I have a tragic vision. I enjoy life. I'm a natural enjoyer. I might have done a bit more dancing. I might have had singing training, but I certainly have no regrets that I chose this course. Well, it chose me.'

He means writing. Still, he knows he did things wrong. There's another poem of his called 'Sentenced to Life', published at the same time as the one about the maple tree, in which he describes himself shuffling down the street in sickness: 'A sad man, sorrier than he could say.' Is that true?
'Yes.'

His sin was to be faithless, says the poem. As if he could be true to everyone at once, 'and all the damage that was done'. So what does he say in his own defence?

'I do have all the standard defensive strategies of the weak artist. I can say betrayal, confusion, weakness, greed, all these things are not unknown in the history of the arts. Very few artists are complete people. If they were, they wouldn't do these things.'

He chuckles to himself, again, perhaps realising how self-excusing he sounds. 'That statement, by the way, is sounding a little gloomy to me. Some people near me, especially my wife and daughters, have heard all that bullshit before.'

Now Clive tells me that his daughter lives next door. His wife and other daughter live across the River Cam, just ten minutes' walk away. He was living in a basement when he got thrown out by Prue, but this quiet two-up two-down has been adapted for him on her orders, with the bright and airy conservatory that doubles as a library. He goes upstairs only to sleep now. Given how close they all seem, geographically, has he been forgiven? 'It's not for me to reach that conclusion, but the evidence is building. I must have something to me. One of the reasons I'm grateful for this extra time is that I've been able to think about my track record and bring it to some sort of conclusion and be grateful that I'm a better man than before I got sick.'

His daughter Claerwen has described him as both a showman and a recluse. 'She got it exactly right. She's sharp as a whip that one.' But she also says his close acquaintance with death has changed him, enormously. 'I've got more time for them, more time for her and for everyone. And I must be more considerate. I was bound to be, incidentally. I couldn't have been worse, before. I was like a lot of driven people. I made that an excuse for not stopping to listen.' Now he's had time to do so. 'What a break that is, eh?'

It can't last forever. Is he scared?

'No. That much I've got going for me. I'm not afraid of death at all, not afraid of not being here. I'm not being heroic when I say I'm not scared. It's all been an adventure and it has been a blessing to have the extra time. I've never written better, because my mind has never been clearer or with fewer distractions. I don't like the idea of the actual dying very much, but it's been a pretty smooth run so far. I daresay I'll get taken away in some quiet manner.' He mentions his writing hero Philip Larkin, the poet. 'He couldn't imagine a world without him. I easily can. I've got that to my advantage. I'm certain that all the heaven and hell I need to bother about and will ever know is here on earth. I wasn't afraid before I was born.'

Clive James has been an atheist for a long time, but I know from his writing that he admires certain people of faith. Is there any sign of him changing his mind about God now? 'No. If there was a supreme being, he would have intervened. He would have come to Auschwitz at Christmas when the snow was falling. He never did,' he says. 'No, of course there's no beyond. This is beyond. We're already there.'

*   *   *

Clive wants to read a poem he has written about his own funeral, which he hopes will one day provide the words inscribed on a plaque at Dawes Point in Sydney Harbour, close to the international shipping terminal, with the first line: 'Here I began and here I reach the end.' He starts, then stumbles. 'No, I've screwed it. Let's do it again.'

Then Clive James begins to read and the strength of his voice returns and for a moment he's the cocksure Aussie with the quick tongue again; the brilliant young man from Kogarah who left on a ship to become one of the cleverest, wittiest commentators in Britain and who was a force in our culture for such a long time but who knows, for sure, that the end is near and it will soon be time for his ashes to be scattered close to where he once departed that Australian life for this, and as the poem says, to 'sink from sight, where once we sailed away'. So what does he think happens next?

'Well, one day in the morning you don't wake up. You don't wake up thinking, "Christ, I'm not here." In that sense Wittgenstein was absolutely right when he said: "Death is not an event in life." '

How about ending it himself? Would that ever be a temptation? I realise it's a crass question, but if I was in his place it would be on my mind.

'If I was in pain, it probably would be. I'm no hero. Either I've got the painless version of whatever it is I've got, or the doctors and scientists are getting very good. Only pain would make me want to do that, and not while I can still write and read and listen to music. I've only just started to listen to music again. I've been saving it up.' He looks across the room and I notice his eyes are glistening. 'My wife and I were sitting here a few months ago on that couch and I was playing her one of the Beethoven late quartets, opus 131, which is a towering work of art. I thought: "Maybe I should be doing this all the time, listening to this." I've only got one eye working. If the time comes when I can't see, I'll start listening to all the old stuff. There's a lifetime of it. I could spend a couple of years just listening to Stravinsky. I'm not going to run out of material.'

And I realise, in this moment, that there is something beautiful and powerful to learn here, from a man who cannot leave his home, whose time is running out, whose life is ending, and whose experience of life is becoming more and more intense as it does, as he has been forced to be still and to make the most of every precious moment, so that the burning colours of the leaves on the Japanese maple tree, the voice of an elegant French stranger, the rise and fall of a string quartet, the company of a lifelong lover who understands and yet forgives him, the capture of an elusive turn of phrase, and the dance of dust motes in a beam of sunlight all give such sweet, exquisite pleasure; not just enjoyment but a sense of joy.

I'm reminded of a musician called Wilko Johnson, who was also in the grip of a terminal illness when I met him and who said in simple terms: 'Nothing makes you feel more alive than being told you are about to die.'

I'd love to find a way to feel like that, to live like that, before it's time to go.

*   *   *

And now, I'm sorry to say, Clive James is dead. He died at home in November 2019. The writer Rachel Cooke, a family friend, visited him just before the end and found their encounter heart-stirring and numinous, to quote words she used in a piece in the *Guardian*. Although she knew he did not believe in the divine, it still seemed present to her.

> When I arrived, he was sitting in the thin autumn sunshine on the little balcony off his sitting room. He had grown a beard, and that, and his happy wave when I came in, made me think of Robinson Crusoe. I was shocked by the way his cancer had ravaged his face – contrary to reports, it wasn't his leukaemia that killed him, but a metastatic squamous cell carcinoma; in other words, it was the Australian sunshine he absorbed in his youth that did for him in the end – but his eyes were refulgent, and he was so full of grace, and so intact in every other way. Somehow, he was the very essence of himself.

She saw what I'd seen but she put it better than I did. Rachel talked to his daughter Claerwen, her good friend, who had spent Clive's final months working with him on a last book called *The Fires of Joy*, a collection of his favourite poems with his thoughts on them, and she said a thing that stays with me, because it puts into the final three words that feeling of intensity, the approach of death revealing a new way to experience life.

'His world had shrunk to this room and that terrace. He never went anywhere, he saw almost nobody, he could eat almost nothing – and yet, every aspect of his life was filled with meaning. The fact that there was an apple on that tree; whether it was rainy or sunny. Everything was extraordinary.'

*   *   *

Learning to Fly

'You wanna fly, you got to give up
the shit that weighs you down.'
Toni Morrison

Kes

Everything *is* extraordinary. Sometimes we stumble across just how true that is. I have been running on empty lately, feeling overwhelmed by everything going on in my life and in the world, so this afternoon I went for a walk. The scientists say something happens when you do that: the chemicals in your body change, so does your mood and the thought processes in your head. I know this to be true: that out in the open air, striding through the natural world, walking the ache out of my legs and filling my air with lungs, I feel different. My shoulders drop. Something unlocks in me. I remember feeling it first as a moody teenager stomping out of our family home, overreacting to something or other my sister did or said and heading for the football fields behind the estate, to find a bit of space on the churned-up pitches, under the widening sky. The grass and the sky were elemental, when so much in life was not. Out on the fields, despite the dog dirt underfoot and the traffic fumes drifting over from the North Circular Road, there was room to breathe.

These days I head for the hills near our home in search of space, light and clarity, so that's where I went today when it all got a bit too much. One of my sons came with me and so did the dog, whose name is Mabel. The three of us were up on a ridge overlooking the town when Josh spotted a bird of prey hovering in mid-air above some bushes, just to the left of the path, about fifty feet in front of us. He said it was a kestrel. I didn't have a clue. The closest I had come to one of those before was watching the movie *Kes*. But I was so struck by the beauty of the moment we were in that I did something that comes naturally to so many of us these days: I whipped out my phone and took a picture. Or rather tried to, because capturing the magic of that scene turned out to be impossible. I ended up with half a dozen photos of a speck. It was so frustrating, but after a while I had no choice but to give up trying and put the phone in my pocket. I was still mesmerised by the bird though and found myself just standing there, slowly becoming more aware of what was going on around me. I heard the kerfuffle of the kestrel's wings and noticed the colours in the sky behind it: soft pinks and dying blues, flashes of green and flecks of gold. I felt the wind and became aware of the breathing of the dog and the presence of my son beside me, with the buttery sunlight on his face. And it was beautiful. I was suddenly, completely there. I felt out of my body and almost weightless, as if I was in the air myself, flying.

Now you might say it was just a bird. You'd be right, but that bird was in perfect harmony with its surroundings, thoroughly able to be itself as it hung in the sky, trusting the wind to lift its wings and waiting for its moment. Flying free. By focusing so hard on the kestrel, I had accidentally allowed myself to be fully swept up in the moment too. I felt something that humans have felt from time to time as long as we have been on the earth and which is described in many different ways in many different faiths, paths and traditions: a connection to something precious and enduring, bigger than myself or any of my problems and certainly way beyond my control. We may not think so but we are all caught up in the same mystery, all connected in the same mysterious way. There have been times in my life when I was certain about what to call the divine and how to make an approach, but the older I get the less I know and the more I am left with a sense of wonder. The Edwardian writer Eden Phillpotts looked at a plant through a magnifying glass, saw intricate beauties that had previously been hidden and wrote: 'The universe is full of magical things patiently waiting for our wits to grow sharper.' He was caught up in wonder and so was I that day, as the sun sank and the light changed and the bird hovered. The world shifted a little. The evening turned out not to be about the walk or even the bird and certainly not about taking a photograph. None of that mattered as much as the sudden, surprising feeling of deep connection to the kestrel, the sky and the wind and the land and the dog and my son, each of us bound together in some way that I am only beginning to understand, but which briefly felt powerful and true.

All the worries have come crashing back since then, of course; but I do feel different now for having had a reminder that beyond the noise of life, the stress and the pain there is beauty waiting to be found, even in things as yet unnoticed like a bird with a name unknown, hanging in mid-air.

*   *   *

Why am I telling you this now? Because the world is full of wonder and we explore that through stories, which also have the power to make and remake our lives. The next few chapters are about exactly that. We will spend them in the company of a couple of fine storytellers, a son of mine and the greatest poet of our age. We begin in the far west of Ireland, way out in the wild Atlantic sea, where a strange song is being carried on the wind.

*   *   *

Seamus

A man plays a slow tune in a lonesome place, one string at a time on the fiddle. He's up late with a dying fire, with his wife asleep and the wind fussing around their stone home, high on the back of the southern Inis. The two of them are the only people on the island of Inishvickillaun, way out in the ocean beyond the far west coast of Ireland. There's nothing to see through the small, deep-set window but the black of night. Nothing to hear but the fizz of the fire, the woman's breath, the wind and another sound he doesn't notice at first as he plays, coming as it does from outside, from above and beside and beyond and away. It's only when Daly stops to rub the back of his bow hand with his other stiff and weary fingers that he hears it and feels a chill at his neck. A female voice, but how can that be? Out in the night, somehow. One long mournful note, then a falling, twisting refrain like the wringing of hands or a wandering mind. A cry of sorrow, loss, climbing, climbing, seeking rest, then tumbling down. It blows away on the wind and Daly holds his breath until it returns, at first barely, then beside him in the room, strong and real, as if being sung for him alone in this place, and no one else, ever. His body resonates with the pure, clear sound.

Over and over the song is sung by the invisible woman, wordless and wonderful, until the fiddler's arms unfreeze and his fingers feel for the bow. Breathless and alive, heart hammering, he pulls notes from the air – now following, now anticipating the flight of the melody as it glides, then beats its wings, then glides again, out in the night and in the room with him, without and within. He plays a line and the singer seems to answer. Again. Again. Until the night begins to lift, light grows within the stones and the music becomes faint. And stops. But Daly has it in him now.

All through the struggles of daytime, the life of man and woman tending sheep on the bare back of an island, the tune does not leave him. He won't let it. Late in the evening, when the fire is covered and the woman sleeps again, the fiddler shoulders his instrument and plays, hoping the singer will return.

She never does.

And yet.

And yet.

And then.

One night on the greater island, back among his people, he plays the tune and tells how it came to him, embroidering the detail and relishing the attention. Others listen carefully and think: 'That's good. I'll have it so.' They ask him to play again and they memorise the melody as he does; and in time they take it with them to the mainland, to the homes of relatives and to bars filled with strangers; and there they conjure their own accounts of its origin. One says it came to his mother as she sat on a stone and looked out to sea. Another says he was in bed with his wife when he heard it and the pair of them sat bolt upright with fright at first, until they realised the singer meant no harm. A third says there are words. They don't fit the tune, but this is spirit music, sung by a tongue that has been silent for too long: 'I am a woman who has come to you from among the faerie people, who has come by wind and wave. It was by night that I was stolen far away, to live with them. I am wandering this earth again by the grace of faerie women, but it is only for a time. When the cock crows I must leave this world behind, in sorrow.'

The tune becomes well known: at first in the town of Dingle, then across Ireland, as it travels on foot, by horse and cart, by boat and train and eventually motorcar. It is passed on, as these things are, from player to player, from session to session, country to country, wherever the Irish gather. It crosses the Atlantic unseen on a steamer and is heard by men with money in their eyes and recorded onto wax, then vinyl, then tape, in studios through time; and every time the tune is a little different, the phrasing changes, the story evolves. And here comes a boy called Seamus to join our tale, growing up in the countryside of County Derry in the 1940s, the eldest of nine children, with the war to them a distant rumble.

'We crowded together in the three rooms of a traditional thatched farmstead and lived a kind of den-life which was more or less emotionally and intellectually proofed against the outside world,' he will one day say, in an acceptance speech for a great prize.

It was an intimate, physical, creaturely existence in which the night sounds of the horse in the stable beyond one bedroom wall mingled with the sounds of adult conversation from the kitchen beyond the other. We took in everything that was going on, of course – rain in the trees, mice on the ceiling, a steam train rumbling along the railway line one field back from the house – but we took it in as if we were in the doze of hibernation.

The earth shook every time a train passed, but the air was alive and signalling too, the wind stirring an aerial wire that came down from the branches of a chestnut tree, through a hole bored in the window to the back of a wireless set. The haze and crackle of static would suddenly give way to the urgent tones of Morse code saying something unknown to someone far away, or the sound of a BBC presenter, sharing the news with the voice of privilege, taken as authority. The names of bombers and of cities bombed, as Heaney would put it. The casualties suffered and the advances made by the Allies and the enemy. And sometimes there would be an adventure story for the boy to relish, with Dick Barton as the hero, or the flying ace Biggles. And the young Seamus would bend close to the wireless and in his concentrated state he would read the names of foreign radio stations written on the dial, including Leipzig, Oslo, Warsaw and Stockholm.

All this is gleaned from an acceptance speech he gave in that Swedish city in 1995 after being given the Nobel Prize. But we're getting ahead of ourselves. The point is that the boy plucked words and meaning and emotion from the air in much the same way as Daly had taken his tune. They were carried on the wind, now fading and now returning with strength, like the song of the spirit woman herself. The young man's habit of writing things down placed him in an ancient tradition, as far as his neighbours were concerned. He told me that as we stood together one night in a bare, backstage room at the Barbican.

'If you take the word "poet" in English, there is an element of the archaic and the prophetic around it,' said Seamus Heaney, who was at that moment probably the most famous poet in the world. 'There is some of that in Irish, but there is also more of what we might think of as the local poet's role: to make up stories and ballads.'

His voice was rich, still energised by a performance he had given earlier, out there on the stage in front of thousands. 'The farmers would say, in a bantering way – and they would still say this to me now – "Watch out for that fellow, he'll put you into a poem." That is a deep traditional memory. Being put into a poem is a way of being pointed out. It's a mixture of public enquiry, gossip column and *Private Eye* . . . a way of ridiculing, and also of exposing. I have more and more respect for that tradition the older I get; but I was, so to speak, educated out of it.'

The boy poet won a scholarship to a Roman Catholic boarding school in the city of Derry, which is where he was living, not sleeping, surviving, when the news came that his little brother Christopher had been killed in a road accident at the age of four. The sorrow went deep. Seamus went on to study English language and literature at Queen's University in Belfast and left with a first-class degree and a greater sense of what he was doing on the page, inspired by the flinty, feathery, bloody words of Ted Hughes. He taught for a living and met his future wife Marie, who was also a teacher and a writer and whose work explored Irish myths and legends. Like him she loved the west of Ireland, the landscapes and music and stories. Their son Michael was born in 1966, the year Seamus published his first fistful of poems. Their second boy Christopher, named after his father's lost brother, came into the world two years later as Seamus wrote a second book called *Door into the Dark*. There's a poem towards the end of that collection called 'The Given Note', which begins in a dry-stone hut on the most westerly Blasket as a fiddler claims a tune from the night to learn and share, as if it were a gift to him from who knows where.

The poem says that those who went to the island later to try to hear what the fiddler had heard could only make out strange noises, nothing like his haunting spirit music. As it happens, I once knew a couple of old lads called Sean and Muiris, brothers who had grown up on the Great Blasket and lived together into their eighties in a little cottage on the mainland, still within sight of their island home. They told me, as we sat drinking whiskey by a small peat fire, that the man who caught the tune was Daly and he was known to their relatives, who heard the music from him first hand when he was still wide-eyed with the wonder of it. They thought the inspiration must have been the sound of whales singing under canvas boats, songs amplified by the wood and canvas and broadcast into the wind; or else a seal crying in a cave. Whatever the source of the music, Seamus Heaney told me he thought the legend had a universal resonance. 'When I first heard the story in 1968, I was struck by the fabulous archetypal quality of it. He hears the tune coming in, and he plays, then others go to see if they can hear it, but they can only hear little bits of things. It seemed to me it was at the heart of one of the big subjects of the species, really: the given-ness of art, the gift of music.'

Famous Seamus, as I'd heard him called by my Irish friends, peered over glasses that had fallen halfway down his nose. The wisps of white hair gathered over his forehead like a sea mist, but grew into turning waves at his temples. This was 1999, we were on the eve of a new millennium and Heaney was rightly known as one of the poets of the century. He was sixty years old but looked timeless. In a tweed jacket and knitted tie, with his face slightly flushed by the warmth of the room and wearing a mischievous smile that seemed to be habitual, he could have been a favourite uncle after a good Sunday lunch. And like an uncle with tales of glories gone by, his question was rhetorical.

'Where do stories come from?'

He asked the wall as if addressing an audience, but I was the only person in the room. I had met him briefly once before and was thrilled to be in his company again for a proper conversation, but anxious to live up to the encounter and to my half-held sense that we might share a sensibility somehow, a way of grasping after meaning and seeing the magical in the ordinary. That was hugely presumptuous of me, but I was a young man and as yet unaware of some of the invisible boundaries of life. Unaware at that point too of the full power and potency of the stories I had spent the last five years collecting in the far west of Ireland, wandering the coastline at the tip of the Dingle peninsula and sitting with the men and women who had once lived on the Great Blasket, several miles out in the Atlantic and now all but abandoned. The last permanent residents had been evacuated in 1953, island life having become too hard. Sean and Muiris were among them. Most of the community had already left over the course of the previous century anyway; one by one, brothers, sisters, lovers, friends and others took the boat, the train, the boat and the train again to Massachusetts, where fate and luck and a strong instinct for mutual self-preservation brought them back together in a place called Hungry Hill. You could have walked down the streets there in the fifties and heard only Irish spoken, and Blasket Irish at that. I had been to meet those emigrants, now elderly, and found in them a sense of being suspended in mid-air, somewhere over the mid-Atlantic: not quite belonging in America, no matter how hard they had tried; always dreaming of the island but knowing that the old life was over. There was no home left for them back there.

I had tried to do them justice in a book called *Hungry for Home* whose title reflected the longing in them – and in me, which is why I was so fascinated with them. And in the course of doing all that, I had come across the tune and the tale, the retelling of a moment that had happened in the 1800s but now, by the magic of storytelling and human connection, linked the wild seas of the far west with the glittering bars of Manhattan and the clapboard homes of Springfield, with the poetry of Seamus Heaney and with the two of us here, in this place, where the great man had just performed a concert with a piper called Liam O'Flynn and read out 'The Given Note', which was based on that famous tune *Port na bPúcaí*. The song of the fairies. I'm not talking about pretty little English Tinkerbells with their gossamer wings and winning smiles. I'm talking about reckless, wandering Irish spirits of the kind who live in the shadows and the hedgerows, on the hills and in the sea foam and cry out in the night. The composer David Bruce, who arranged the tune for violin, cello, guitar, clarinet and bass wrote of 'The Given Note': 'I understand Heaney's beautiful poem to be a meditation on the unfathomable origins of all music, all art, all inspiration. In a way they are "given" to us from somewhere mysterious, and although in the modern world we might laugh at the quaint concept of "fairies", when you think about the intangible origins of art, perhaps the idea isn't so wide of the mark.'

The writer Kurt Vonnegut put it another way, saying: 'If I should ever die, God forbid, let this be my epitaph: the only proof he needed for the existence of God was music.' Music is definitely something we can't see that touches us deeply, something we barely understand that moves us beyond thought. Something so much more than the sum of its parts, the technical details of marks on a page, fingers on strings, hammering keys and even vocal cords vibrating. Something elusive, but undeniably powerful.

Seamus Heaney found other connections in Daly's ethereal duet.

'The sound of the mighty wind is a locus classicus of inspiration,' he said to me, speaking carefully, like a patient don giving a tutorial. 'It comes into Christian mythology at Pentecost with the rushing wind that preceded the descent of the tongues of flame. I linked it in my own mind to the story of the German poet Rainer Maria Rilke in the tower at Duino, going out into a storm and hearing his big music, from which he was able to finish the *Duino Elegies* and then write the *Sonnets to Orpheus*.'

I nodded, as if to affirm and encourage, although I had never heard of Rilke and had no idea where Duino was.

Seamus said: 'Even the great bad poet of the nineteenth century William McGonagall tells the story of his own origins as a poet and says: "It was as if I heard a mighty wind, and out of the wind a voice saying: 'Write, write'."'

I've looked up William McGonagall since then and in this context his quote can be taken as a parody of all those who claim inspiration from God in the midst of a storm.

When we met that time in the Barbican Seamus Heaney was on tour with Liam O'Flynn, trading words and tunes with the piper and in the process taking Daly's private island music to the concert halls of the great cities of Europe and America. 'The story is so attractive because it has the high voltage of tradition in it. The music itself is beguiling, and impossible to describe.' Maybe it really was the song of a spirit mourning her fate. Maybe it was the sound of a seal weeping in a cove. Or the cry of a hump-backed whale swimming underneath a boat. Or perhaps there is a clue in *The Western Island*, a book by the writer Robin Flower, a friend of many Blasket islanders. Writing in the 1930s, he describes how the wireless had come to the community and brought news from the outside world, vivid tales that crowded out the old stories and called the young men and women to leave. For him, the song that Daly heard was symbolic and resonant as 'a lament for a whole world of imaginations, banished irrevocably now'.

*   *   *

When Seamus became world famous he was on another island somewhere in the Peloponnese, the part of Greece in which Hercules fought a lion long ago, Helen of Troy eloped with Paris and the Argonauts set sail in search of the Golden Fleece. This was 1995, before the widespread use of mobile phones and the coming of the internet and the constant, insistent arrival of messages and alerts. The poet had been out of contact with the world for a few days, happily holidaying with his wife Marie and two of their friends, when he wandered over to a landline telephone to check in with his son Christopher, who was back at home in Ireland that Friday afternoon.

Christopher said: 'Did you hear?'

The poet, puzzled, said: 'No.'

'You've won the Nobel Prize.'

'Come on!'

He thought his son was kidding, but it was true. And when a reporter came all the way from Ireland to interview him for television a few days later, Seamus Heaney looked bashful in his white summer cotton shirt, with his white bushy eyebrows and snowy hair, like Santa Claus beardless on vacation. 'It's entirely bewildering,' he said with an enigmatic smile. 'It's an awesome dimension of a thing to have happened.'

Then Seamus was asked to say a poem of his own that would mean something in the moment and there was one he knew by heart; about how, as a boy, he had sat with his mother peeling potatoes for the Sunday roast, bending over the bowl of cold water into which the spuds would go with a splash, their two heads almost touching, as close as they would ever be for the whole of their lives. A reminder of who and what he had been.

*   *   *

There was hope in his home country when Seamus Heaney stood up to give his Nobel acceptance speech, but nervousness too. The Good Friday Agreement had been signed the year before and nobody was really sure if it would hold. What do you say when they give you a prize like that at a time like that? Seamus found a way to make the personal and the local say something about the national and the international. He talked about having been bent double by the Troubles, trying to hammer words into hard meanings to match the times. And then, as he put it: 'I straightened up. I began a few years ago to try to make space in my reckoning and imagining for the marvellous as well as for the murderous.' And there in the hall in Stockholm he told a story out of Ireland. It could have come from India or Africa or the Arctic or the Americas, he said, which was not to dismiss it as a folk tale but to suggest it was worth sharing, and trusting and thinking about, precisely because it came from a time and a place and a people; and the telling would share something of who they were, what they meant and what they wanted. Who he was. What he meant. He was working away at the story in private, making a poem from it, although nobody in the grand room knew that. Here, then, was a simple story from home.

Kevin was a monk who lived in the woody, watery landscape of County Wicklow. He was said to have been born in the year 498 and his name suggested a noble family. He must have wanted to get away from people though, because he lived in a cave, as a hermit. Not just any old cave but one cut specially into a rock face, about thirty feet up, overlooking a lake. The cave still exists and is known as St Kevin's Bed, which sounds right as there is not enough room to stand up in it. Seamus didn't say this but there's also a legend that he was pursued by a woman who took a fancy to him and would not take no for an answer. He slept badly, dreaming that she was on top of him in the cave, riding him. And when he woke up, Kevin found that it was true. Half asleep but alarmed, he pushed her off and she fell out of the cave, thirty feet down into the water, and drowned.

I have no idea if that's true, but it doesn't sound like any way for a saint to behave.

This barefoot, wild-eyed, long-haired holy man became famous, despite himself. So famous that when Ireland's greatest living poet stood up to accept the highest praise and prize a person of letters can obtain, he told another tale of Kevin. This time the saint was kneeling in prayer with his arms stretched out in the form of a cross. As he did so, for hour after hour, a blackbird mistook the still, upturned palm for a good place to nest. The bird brought twig after twig and patches of moss and after a while, when all was settled, there were eggs. Still Kevin did not move, despite what must have been the agony, for fear of disturbing the bird. Or as Seamus Heaney put it in his speech, he was 'overcome with pity and constrained by his faith to love the life in all creatures great and small'.

Kevin kept his arms outstretched until the eggs vibrated and cracked and fledglings emerged and grew wings and became bigger and stronger and blacker and flew. None of this makes sense, does it? That's kind of the point, said Heaney. The story is at the intersection of what we know and believe to be true and what could be true, a signpost to another way of seeing. And of course, it is all made up anyway.

That's how Seamus put it when he published a poem called 'St Kevin and the Blackbird', the year after the Nobel Prize. In it he wonders if there was great pain in Kevin's fingers, his back, his neck and his knees, or whether the future saint was numb and forgot himself, his body lost in prayer as much as his mind. Forgetting himself, forgetting the river by which he knelt, forgetting even the bird.

Heaney means something more than pins and needles here. The poem talks of Kevin 'finding himself linked to the network of eternal life'. So many faiths, paths, traditions and communities share the idea that it is possible for humans to experience moments of profound harmony, when we feel at one with everyone and everything, as I did that day with the kestrel. Lord knows those times are hard to come by, though. Perhaps poetry, imagination and story are the best tools we have to describe what may be going on. It lies beyond our theories, rules, theologies and laws, at a point at which we admit we know very little and are honestly mostly just scrabbling about in the dark. Flying by the seat of our pants. Making it up as we go along. Once you get that, it is easier to stay kneeling and holding out your hand, I think. Easier to see past religions and institutions and all their incompetence and cruelty and feel there is something out there and within us which stands for beauty and love and a higher power. Easier to forget yourself and feel at one with the world, if you're lucky.

I have a print on my wall that was made by a Scottish artist and bought for me by a friend, which shows the blackbird's nest in one of St Kevin's upturned palms. That's because for me the story represents something close to what another saint called Francis named as the great chain of being. We are each of us connected intimately to the natural world around us, whether we know it or feel it or not. We do our best to become aware of that and act accordingly, or so the saints say. When you think of climate change, and the reason we are in this mess, they have a point. I find it helpful to think of a piece of music playing behind everything we do, a song that once heard can never be unheard, which is the song of the genuine, the song of the energy that binds us, the song of the divine, whatever we choose to call it. The writer Brian McLaren uses the same language to describe the connection with the universe that humans long for and which he believes is the experience at the core of all or most religions. He writes: 'This coming-into-union, this encounter-without-judgment, this knowing-without-control goes from me to you to us and beyond, to plants and animals and all of the created world. We come to hear the same music, the sound of the genuine flowing through everything, every thing, every thing.' He insists that all this is as available to us all as easily as wind, rain and sun. 'It is here. Available. At hand. Within reach. Right now.'

This is all metaphorical, you might say; but sometimes metaphor is all we have. A thought or a story. They have power, those things. Stories carry values and meaning down the ages, from mouth to ear to mouth. So in Stockholm, in front of the Nobel jury, Seamus Heaney told his tale of Ireland. In his new telling, it had meaning and resonance again.

'I hope I am not being sentimental or simply fetishising the local,' he said that night. 'I wish instead to suggest that images and stories of the kind I am invoking here do function as bearers of value. The century has witnessed the defeat of Nazism by force of arms; but the erosion of the Soviet regimes was caused, among other things, by the sheer persistence, beneath the imposed ideological conformity, of cultural values and psychic resistances of a kind that these stories and images enshrine.'

Seamus Heaney was certainly part of the resistance, with his ability to write about a wild old saint and a bird or peeling potatoes and make the meaning encompass so much more including war, anguish and love. When I asked him about that in the Barbican in 1999, he replied by asking and answering his own question. 'Where do stories come from? You take them to be pre-natal possessions,' he said, suggesting that we are born into them. 'They situate you in a culture, or a world.'

This is true. The stories I was born into may be different from the ones you know. Some of them are shared among us, like Cinderella or Aladdin or these days the myths and legends of the Marvel Cinematic Universe, designed as they are to promote their own particular set of American values; but there are others that are particular to my people, my time and place or yours. 'The story of the music out of the wind reminds me of that phrase of Wordsworth in *The Prelude* about the relationship between the individual consciousness and the cosmos itself,' Seamus told me, musing aloud like an old academic don again as he looked to the door and possibly thought about leaving, going back to his wife and friends. 'He describes the child as "An inmate of this *active* universe". A story mediates between cosmos and consciousness: it makes the individual child, or listener, an inmate of an older, longer, deeper, more linked-up system.' What exactly did he mean by a story? 'I mean fairy tale and the traditional inheritance – the lump of stuff that is carried around. I mean that which the group has put into the kitbag of memory.'

I liked that description and told him so, then found myself clumsily trying to get us back on solid ground by saying: 'I have a story in my kitbag that's about you.'

'Oh yes, what's that?'

'It's about when we met before. Do you remember?'

'I'm sorry,' he said, looking wary. 'I don't recall . . .'

'That's okay,' I said. 'You've had a lot going on.'

So I told him the story. Thankfully, he laughed.

*   *   *

I first met Seamus Heaney on a warm day in 1996, a few months after he had been given the big prize. We were in Cambridge, at a college chapel where a service was held to remember a friend of mine and of his, the great poet and critic and Yorkshireman Donald Davie. I was half a century younger than Donald but had written to him after reading *To Scorch or Freeze*, a collection of poems in which he attempted to rework the Psalms in modernist style. This was quite a departure for a poet who had made his name in the fifties as a contemporary of Philip Larkin in the Movement and was best known for precise, terse, ordered verse, bounded by rules. Here he was writing fractured lines about the mesmer-ising bowling motion of the cricketer Imran Khan, for exam-ple, or the frozen beauty of the Arctic. Flying from Britain to America over those ice floes and glittering white plains, it struck him that they might be something like the presence of God: gorgeous to witness, breathtaking to be near and inspir-ing to see if you were ready, prepared and properly dressed; but deadly, if you were naked and unaware. This way of thinking put him in touch with an old Celtic idea that heaven and hell might be the same place, in the way that ice can burn your fingers or chill your whisky, depending on how you approach it. He wanted to be ready; perhaps that was part of why he had been baptised at the age of seventy-seven. I found all this fascinating, so I wrote to ask if I could come and see Donald Davie down in Devon. I was only an undergraduate, studying English literature, but he allowed me to visit and even picked me up from Exeter station in his cardigan and carpet slippers, sucking a pipe. I stayed in a room at his local pub for several days and walked to Donald's house for long, detailed and recorded conversations, punctuated by lunch-time pints or martinis he mixed at home in the late after-noon, or by him taking exception to some particularly crass question about what a particular poem meant, when he would growl: 'Do your own work!'

He would laugh but I knew he meant it. Hard work mattered. This was a man from mining country, who had served in the Navy during the war. We were talking at a time in the early nineties when poetry was a marginal pursuit, seen as something indulgent, archaic or silly, but certainly of little interest to the general public. Not like now, of course: pubs fill up for poetry slams, people pack out venues to hear Kae Tempest declare mesmerising words to music, Stormzy and Little Simz fill stadiums, my friend Pádraig Ó Tuama leads the finest of many podcasts, Carol Ann Duffy and Simon Armitage have been vocal laureates, Michael Rosen and Lemn Sissay are voices of sanity in the national conversation. Back then, nobody much wanted to know. I knew Donald was a late convert to Christianity and had found comfort in the *Book of Common Prayer*, which he said took the pressure off him when he prayed. 'I can use the old words and not feel like I have to try and impress God as a phrasemaker, which is what I do by instinct,' he said. The Church of England was in its own End Times though, we could both see that even then. So how did it feel, I asked with the boldness and arrogance of youth, to be the master of a dying art and the follower of a dying faith? He growled again, of course. 'Neither of those things make a difference. Just because a thing is not popular does not mean it is of less value.'

I loved him then for clinging on, for keeping going, for the art of his words and the belligerence of his approach and for the generosity he was showing me in answering at all. Later, in a letter, he proposed something that took my breath away. 'When I die, there may be some thought of a book about me. I would like you to write it.'

I never did. I was too intimidated. I'm sorry about that now. But I did go along to the memorial service at a college chapel in Cambridge, which was intimate but included a number of notable poets who had been among his friends and admirers. Geoffrey Hill was there with others whose names might not mean much beyond literary circles, but so was the newly named Nobel winner Seamus Heaney. Here was a man whose charm and work was helping to make poetry popular again. I was many decades younger than any of the other writers present and awestruck to be in their company. I was also recently married and my wife had come with me to Cambridge, but gone shopping rather than attend the service, having no interest in poetry at all. She caught up with us afterwards, wandering into the circle of greats with no knowledge of any of them, including Seamus, who stopped in mid-anecdote when he saw the young beauty arrive, turned quickly and drawled his greeting, like a Celtic Leslie Phillips: 'Hello, my dear . . .'

He must have been greeted with warmth and adoration so often since his win, but it didn't happen this time. Rachel smiled and returned his greeting politely, like a bridesmaid dismissing a tipsy uncle at a wedding, then turned away to get herself a glass of wine. She had absolutely no idea who he was, that was obvious. Famous Seamus looked crushed, but only briefly. Then he realised he was being watched, worked out what she was doing there and turned to me with that internationally renowned, enigmatic smile.

'Ah, well. At least you'll have a story . . .'

* * *

Philip

You're tired and hungry. You've travelled a long way in search of answers and here they are at last, waiting behind a locked door. You're scared, because their keeper is said to be a terrifying creature who rips people's heads off. You knock tentatively, wanting to run away. Too late now, though. The door opens slowly, until the outline of the beast is revealed in the half-light and a voice rumbles like a distant earthquake.

'Come inside . . .'

Do you dare?

Of course you do, because you have to complete your quest; and anyway, this is real life not a fairy tale. Sir Philip Pullman is one of the big beasts of literature and has a reputation for being fierce, that is true, but he doesn't look like anyone's idea of a monster today in his sandals, chinos and white shirt, with his white hair sticking up at eccentric angles. He's at home here in his farmhouse on the edge of a village in the countryside near Oxford and there is actually a gentleness about him, as his dogs sniff around our legs.

'Come through,' he says. 'Let's just clear that chair of books.'

Here in this gloriously cluttered, book-lined study, the author scratches words onto paper with a fountain pen every day. Out they fly into the world then, to land on readers and listeners, getting inside the heads and hearts of boys and girls and men and women, whispering secrets while the author who sent them never has to leave his room. The skill in his pen has made Sir Philip famous and put so much money in the bank I imagine he could actually be a bank now if he wanted to. He has been knighted for his contribution to literature, won the Carnegie Medal and the Whitbread Book of the Year award and created in Lyra, the young subject of the trilogy *His Dark Materials*, a hero of the age to rival Harry Potter or Hermione Granger. 'I started because I thought it would be a fine thing to write a book and I've continued because I discovered there's joy as well,' says Sir Philip, who was a teacher until his forties. 'There's fun in writing. There's delight. There's a solid sense of achievement. There's the clear satisfaction of working out a plot. There's the connection with the reader, ultimately. But one of the basic satisfactions, or necessities, that make it urgent and important is that it stops me from going mad.'

He says this in a matter-of-fact, absolutely certain sort of way that is startling.

'I'm not trying to prove anything to anyone, I'm just trying to stop myself going mad. I am a frail and uncertain being. I'm a congenital melancholic. And if I didn't have a purpose, I'd very quickly begin to think, "Why am I here? What's my point?" My thoughts would turn to rope and branches of trees and poison and kitchen knives and all sorts of things.'

Really? I'm a little taken aback by the ease with which this hugely successful man talks about the danger of falling into thoughts of suicide. His wife is in the kitchen next door. Here in the study that is his personal domain he has his mug of tea, his books, an electric piano he can play and a guitar that he can't really, yet. He answers every question thoughtfully and carefully, but seems fascinated with life rather than unhappy. Suicide is not a thing to be spoken of lightly, so I have to ask, does he really mean it?

'I am serious about that, yeah. I could very easily fall into that state of mind. But working as I do is a kind of defence against that, because I can say, "At least I'm doing something here. I'm not just taking up space." '

We have met before, as it happens: ten years ago at the South Bank in 2008, when he was helping a friend launch a comic for children. I knew his reputation for being curmudgeonly like one of those mighty armoured polar bears in his stories, but he was very gracious in letting my son interview him for the *Independent*. Jacob was eleven years old then, but Sir Philip spoke to him as an equal. The teacher in him remains strong, and he continues to campaign for better schools, but let's cut to the chase: these are troubled times, so what good are mere stories now?

'My answer is the one given by Samuel Johnson: "The true aim of writing is to enable the reader better to enjoy life, or better to endure it." Some books are priceless entertainment when you're in a dreadful situation. You've just been diagnosed with a terrible disease. You're frightened. Or your spouse has, or your children. But you can endure it if you've got something comfortable to read that brings you release, consolation, that sort of thing. P. G. Wodehouse, for example.' Sir Philip understands that situation, having recently been through an operation. It's hard to say how well he is as we're just sitting around the house but his voice and mind are strong. 'I like to think I would be writing exactly the same words in exactly the same way if I was now a retired teacher, struggling to live on a pension. I would still go to my desk. In fact, I'd have more time, because I wouldn't be gadding about so much.'

He's best known for *His Dark Materials*, in which Lyra and her daemon (an animal extension of the soul) called Pan battle for the truth against an oppressive religious authority called The Magisterium, running into quite a few armoured polar bears. As we speak, he is working on the second book of a follow-up trilogy, which is collectively known as *The Book of Dust*. I've read that the trilogy will be worth £8 million in sales for Waterstones alone. Does he feel any pressure about that as he sits down to write? 'None at all. Partly because I've got plenty of money myself, so whether the next one bombs or sells a million is of no concern to me whatsoever. I'm extraordinarily lucky. Besides, I'm an old man now. Fifty years in this game. I can shut these things out.'

The book he is writing is called *The Secret Commonwealth* and again tells the story of Lyra, now grown up and trying to come to terms with the loss of childhood wonder. What is the secret commonwealth of the title? 'It's the world of imagination, of shadows, fancies, dreams, ghosts, memories. And it's just not accessible to rationality, reason or scientific method. This trilogy is about growing up, so I'm describing what happens when we lose our apprehension of the secret commonwealth as we get older. Is it gone forever? How do we cope in a world that we no longer feel has any magic in it?'

Is this secret commonwealth real or does it just exist in fiction? 'This atmosphere, this vision, whatever it is, is one of the most important things about us, because it enables us to work or not to work. And by work, I mean creation work.'

This seems to indicate a change in his thinking. Sir Philip has long been seen as a champion of atheism, a flag-bearer for the rational and scientific, but he agrees that this no longer satisfies him. 'Rationalism, though mighty and great and the source of enormous benefit to human beings – both scientific and technological, societal, whatever – is not the only way of seeing things. No work of art was ever reasoned into existence, for example. My entire life has been based around art of one sort or another, since I was a schoolboy, so I know full well that if I had to depend on rationality, it wouldn't get done.'

Rationality is not sufficient for life, in his opinion, but it is still important.

'If we abandon rationality in society, before we know where we are we're like Donald Trump and we're welcoming in a new Dark Age,' he says, because this is the summer of 2018 and there is a madman in the White House. 'So rationality has a very important, an honourable and necessary place, but it has limits. If you exalt it to something more then you quickly find yourself talking about eugenics: "It's not rational that we should breed people who are not fit. Let's get rid of them." That's one of the consequences of extreme rationalism without any tempering by emotion, imagination, empathy. I want to restore these other things.' Hearing this I wonder if he minds having been grouped so often with the militant new atheists like Richard Dawkins, an altogether more arrogant, less gracious man? 'Not at all. People only have to read me to see the difference.'

Okay, let me take this further. Does the idea of the secret commonwealth mean he could ever see himself taking a step towards any kind of faith in anything other than the rational? 'Well I think that very question poses another question, which is: "What's faith got to do with rationality?" If you're rational, you base your life on what is reasonable to believe,' he says in a patient tone, the teacher in him beginning to rise. 'It's reasonable to believe that the postman will come tomorrow because it's a Friday and he comes on a Friday. It's not reasonable, if you're rational, to believe that if you're a bad person, very wicked, you'll go to hell and be tormented forever.'

No, but neither is it reasonable to believe in elves, fairies and folklore and other aspects of the secret commonwealth that he explores and celebrates in his stories, is it? 'No, that's my point. If you live your life according only to reason, you won't see that side of life. You won't be able to either appreciate or create art of any kind.' Really? He pauses to think about that for a moment. 'Though Richard Dawkins appreciates art. He appreciates music. He loves the *St Matthew Passion* and so on. So there must be a side of him that is not entirely governed by reason. I think he'd probably say that was true.'

Still, this secret commonwealth of his exists in the same kind of territory as faith, doesn't it? 'Yes it does,' he says, smiling. 'But my answer is I don't mind what you believe. I've never objected to you believing anything. What I object to is when you start ordering me around, in political terms, for no other reason than that God has told you to do so. That's where the problems are. When religion and politics start holding hands, watch out.'

He explored the ambiguities of this in his book *The Good Man Jesus and the Scoundrel Christ*, with its opening sentence that challenged those with a conventional understanding of the Gospels right from the start: 'This is the story of Jesus and his brother Christ: of how they were born, of how they lived and how one of them died. The death of the other is not part of the story.' The Jesus in the book is an attractive but misguided idealist who cannot help praying to a God he knows is absent. His twin brother Christ is weak and sly and shifts the meaning of stories, sexing up potential miracles in the name of what a mysterious stranger tells him is a truth beyond history. Some Christians were offended, but others enjoyed the book hugely, responding to the very clear direction on the back cover that said: 'This is a story.' Like *Monty Python's Life of Brian* and the movie *The Last Temptation of Christ*, Sir Philip's *The Good Man Jesus and the Scoundrel Christ* is a work of art that has inspired a knee-jerk, outraged, censorious response from some people of faith but been a pleasure to others, for its own sake and because it asks us to think again about what we believe.

'I wrote a thought experiment for the afterword of that book,' he says. 'I'd like to ask Christians to do this. Imagine yourself back in Jerusalem, in those last three days or so of Jesus's life. Imagine that you can see him as he goes about, upsetting the money changers in the temple, speaking, preaching. And you know that in three days he'll be betrayed and put to a terrible death, a most appalling, ghastly death. Now, imagine also that you've got the power, if you want to use it, to embrace him, much as Judas did, and magically send him away to somewhere where he'd be safe: Alexandria, Babylon, Bombay, somewhere he wouldn't be executed. But there would be no Church. Would you do it? Would you save his life or not?' It's an excellent question. What do Christians say? 'I don't know because it's only been written down so far. I've never actually put the question to anyone in person.'

Silence falls, as it takes me a moment to realise that he's asking me, here and now. Okay then, let's think. I would save the life of Jesus, I say.

'Any decent person would.'

This is getting personal now. I am a follower of Jesus, in the sense that I am fascinated by the man and what he stood for and the way he lived and who he claimed to be. I used to say I had a personal relationship with him and I think that's still true, because when I reach out to the divine it is often through him, but as they say about relationships these days, it's complicated. I was born into Christianity. I had no choice about that. My grandparents were in the Salvation Army. My father rebelled against their way of life and became a socialist, although his politics and those of the Labour Party had been formed and informed by Christianity too, so there was little escape for me there. I duly fell for the rebel Jesus, the man in the stories who ate with outcasts, knelt down to children, stood in front of a mob that was to kill a woman with stones and told them to throw the first stone if they had done nothing wrong. The man who overturned the temple tables in rage, who rode into town on a donkey to satirise the king who had ridden there on a beautiful white horse, the man who turned everything upside down in the way he was and the things he said. Him. I fell for him. I'm still fascinated by him. I'm as appalled as Philip Pullman by some of the things that have been done in his name, or by people exploiting faith, including power grabs and empires, palaces and fortunes built on the back of someone who said to take nothing with you when you go, who told the rich man who came secretly at night to give up everything he owned in order to become free. All of this was my inheritance, by accident of birth. I could have been in love with the Buddha, in awe of Allah or a follower of some other path, some other creed, some other faith or tradition, but as it happens the life of Jesus was the beginning point for me, the set of stories that opened up the doors of my thinking and feeling and let me enter into the search for meaning and the divine and that which lies beyond. I chose to embrace that in my life but I have also grown to see wisdom and love and community and meaning in other stories too, other faiths and among people of no faith. We are all humans, trying to make sense of it all.

We do that with stories. They change us. They build us. They knock the edges off us. They help us find out who we are and who we are not. Sharing them creates a connection between us that is powerful and transformative. The story of humanity is in part the story of men and women wondering what to do about those in-between moments when magic breaks into a life we thought was ordinary and gives us a sudden, unexpected sense of being connected and collected up, when a goal is scored or when the crowd sings the big chorus, when the clouds move across the sky, the wind rustles the leaves in the forest canopy or a kestrel catches the eye. The secret commonwealth. The stories we tell about these things change according to who we are and how we understand the world and they also shift over time. 'The spirit that lives in the trees is talking to us,' is one of the things we humans used to say way back in time, and some still do. 'The sun that rises is the bringer of life. The storm on the horizon is a warning from the gods. The wound in my side is a judgement on my life. The plague we are suffering is because of the bad people in our midst.' See how quickly we go dark? How soon stories turn from playfulness and the leap of imagination to self-condemnation or a verdict on others? How quickly rules are formulated, too. 'This is what we mean, let's nail it down, let's get it right so that anyone can understand' becomes something else. 'Let's create rules based on what we know and define who we are and fight for them. Let's die for them. Let's kill for them.'

All this happens so fast in human history and in our own lives, and we take it all so terribly seriously, when actually, as I say, we are just a bunch of people telling stories, trying to understand.

I remember Desmond Tutu suggesting in a book called *God is Not a Christian* that if Jesus is right in what he tells his friends in the Gospels then God is universal and outside of time as well as present in the here and now, and therefore exists way beyond the institutions and stories we've built and called Christianity. If they were not there, the divine would find another way through. It does. Sir Philip nods. 'These questions are always worth talking about, because they do expose all kinds of assumptions that one has.'

I want to know about this secret commonwealth of his, though. Is it all in our heads, or actually present in the world in some way? 'It's in your head, but it also might be partly in the world, because our senses are partly in the world,' he says. 'I've recently been reading Galen Strawson, who is a proponent of panpsychism. That is the doctrine that consciousness doesn't only exist in the human mind, it exists all over the place. Everything is conscious. Consciousness is a normal property in matter, just like mass. I find that very attractive.'

I struggle to quite grasp this in the moment, but there's more.

'I've also been reading someone else whose name has escaped me temporarily, who suggests that the human mind doesn't only exist in the brain, it extends outwards. Part of our mind is in that little bookstand on the table there, because I made that. The care I spent on making it is some-how still in it.' Or the tunes that he might have played on his guitar? 'Exactly. I think the bookstand probably has more of my mind in it than the guitar because I don't play very well. But I spent a lot of time doing it.'

I'm a guitarist, I confess. 'So you know what I mean. So this notion of where the mind is and how far the mind goes out – as we see in Wordsworth's *Prelude*, for example, when he steals the rowing boat and rows out at night on the lake, the big mountain ahead comes into sight and he's suddenly overtaken by a sense of other modes of being. That's the sort of thing I want to explore in *The Secret Commonwealth*.'

'Let's play,' I say, looking for a way to catch hold of all this, and he's startled.

'Pardon?'

'Let's play a tune together.'

'Are you serious?'

'Yes,' I hear myself saying, to my own surprise. So I pick up the guitar and check the tuning, which is only a little off.

He chuckles and moves to the electric keyboard, switching it on and trying out a few, tentative chords. 'I'm only just beginning really but I can keep up with a song.'

We settle on a Tom Waits tune called 'Take It With Me', which I tell him has the most beautiful last verse of lyrics I've ever heard. It's quite simple, a matter of playing C, F, G and Am in various sequences. Sir Philip nods and sets his fingers out in the right places for those chords, reminding himself and off we go. This is all happening spontaneously: we were talking, the interview slipped into a conversation that was enjoyable but in danger of getting away from us both and now here is music, taking our tentative connection beyond words, even if neither of us could be called a virtuoso. Or perhaps it works because we are both a bit clumsy with it. We have to watch each other's movements to stay in time and tune, which is intimate. Nobody else is listening, it's just us. As the last chord resolves, we smile at each other, full beam, grateful for the unexpected pleasure of the moment.

'Thank you,' he says warmly and I am reminded of something he said earlier. 'I'm not Sir Philip Pullman.' That was disconcerting, but I see now that what he meant was that he is not – in himself and to himself – the public figure that people see. 'That's a mask. I have no interest in that sort of thing at all. It's not like the absolute misery of being a rock star or film star. At least I can walk down the street. Occasionally someone will stop me and say, "Excuse me, are you Philip Pullman?" But they don't want to say, "You bastard! What a rotten writer you are." They say, "I enjoyed your book." So that's nice of them. Generally speaking, I am polite back.'

Generally speaking. If you're lucky and you catch him on a good day, he'll be nice to you. I have been lucky, clearly. Sir Philip has been very generous with his time, but I know that what he really wants to do is write. Three pages of A4 a day, no more and no less.

'If you want the muse to visit you, she needs to know where you are. So, my advice is to go to your desk every day and stay there. The habit of being in the same place every day is an enormous help for all sorts of reasons. If you decide that you are going to produce three pages every day, as I have done for fifty years, it does help you overcome those periods when it's difficult. So what if it is? Do it anyway.'

Does he honestly stop writing when he's filled up three pages with his fountain pen, even if it's going well? 'Yes, because you pick it up easily the next day. It's a very good place to stop.' I would be afraid to do that, I say. 'I've done it for fifty years and it works. It's a barrier against being blocked. I hate that phrase.'

He's talking about writer's block, in which Sir Philip does not believe.

'Of course it's difficult sometimes. So is anything. But you didn't think it was going to be easy, did you? So just stay there until you get it done.' When it's hard going he writes dialogue, because that's easier. 'Sometimes, if the evening wears on and I haven't written anything, I resort to a very large wine glass full of gin. It works.'

Sir Philip's eyes skip again to the writing desk. Won't be long now and he can be there again. 'Thank you for keeping going,' I say on behalf of all those he has touched; but the gruff old charmer just smiles as he shows me out and says gently, as if it is almost true: 'Well, it's self-preservation. I'm not doing it for anybody else.'

*   *   *

Jacob

My eldest son Jacob was born at the end of a long and difficult process of our trying to have a child, and his birth was a great blessing to us, in every sense of that word. I am proud to have been involved for many years in the Greenbelt festival of arts, faith and justice and around the time he was born some artists at the event including the Chilean René Castro were taking inspiration from the story of Jacob in the Bible, who apparently wrestled all night with an angel, refusing to let go until he was given a blessing. It's dangerous to take bits of anybody's sacred texts and tack them onto your life, particularly when you're talking about something that may or may not have happened thousands of years ago in a culture you can barely even begin to understand, but I'm not going to lie, there were parallels between the story and what we were going through. So we called our son Jacob, as a nod to that story and the idea that some things are worth struggling for.

I was thinking about that this morning when I came across a piece by a rabbi called René Pfertzel, which really moved me. He works in London but was born in the much disputed territory of Alsace, where his grandparents spoke Alsatian, German and Yiddish. The rabbi says the story of Jacob and the angel refers to a deeper fight, and I want to share his words with you, because they seem to express so much of what I mean to say about how we make and remake ourselves by sharing our stories and listening to others.

It is not only with one human being, but with all the people that live inside him that Jacob wrestled. Like him, we ask ourselves, where is my place in the universe? Where is my place in my family, in my community, in my society? How do I embrace all these people who live inside me? We live indeed in an endless network of connections and relationships that define who we really are. No human being lives in complete isolation, and each encounter changes us forever. Sometimes, we get hurt; sometimes, we get limitations from others. The space where you and I meet is the place of the encounter, and also the place of the transformation. Each conversation we have, each of the people we meet on our journey, each new thought we receive from outside changes us within.

*   *   *

Jacqueline

Once upon a time there was a little girl whose head was full of stories.

She was not great at things like maths and not very good at sport, so people would pick her last for games. They'd rather have anyone else but Little Jackie Daydream, who spent all her time with her face buried in a book or lost in stories of her own making.

This was in the days after the Second World War, when sweets and sweet things were still rationed, and everything looked drab and grey and tired except in a child's imagination. There were arguments at home, Mum and Dad didn't get on, so the little girl would take herself off into a quiet corner and hide in other realities. She was an only child, so Jackie daydreamed about what it would be like to be in a bigger family full of happy noise and love and company. She imagined a teenager who was very full of herself and stayed out late with her boyfriend and worried her mum terribly. Then a rather earnest girl with glasses who loved reading, another girl with plaits who was desperate to be an actress and a mischievous pair of identical twins who kept playing tricks on people. The youngest children in her imaginary family were a shy little boy who got teased and a fierce, funny little girl with an awful lot of curly hair.

Jackie dreamed them up and then she wrote them down in an exercise book and on the cover she drew pictures of them all, including the mum, who had worry lines on her face. And she gave the family a name which fitted the idea of there being lots of them, wriggling about in the tight space of their home. They were called the Maggots. And the little girl showed the book to her teacher, who thought it was funny and smiled when she read the stories; so on the way home Jackie skipped along the pavement, avoiding the cracks and playing a game in her head in which she was a famous writer being interviewed about her work. And sixty years later I am on the way to see her, because Jacqueline Wilson has written more than one hundred books. She's sold more than 40 million copies, met an American president, been made a fellow of the Royal Literary Society and is now a Dame. Very few people have had her kind of influence over the imagination and impulses of the last few generations of British children and therefore, subsequently, adults. And all this because of the ideas and characters that have come from her brain.

'I know,' she is going to say. 'Isn't it weird?'

*   *   *

And now Jacqueline Wilson is standing by the roadside, deep in the English countryside, showing me where to turn the car. The big wooden gate to her estate is open, so I turn left off the road that leads over the Downs to a ridiculously pretty village and instead take the drive that snakes up the hill to her house.

'It's a thirties house, much bigger than I've ever lived in before,' she says, glancing up at the red-brick chimneys. She's a small woman with a powerful presence and her hair is in a kind of Mod mullet, like a bright white Ziggy Stardust. Jackie is wearing black jeans and a big, comfy-looking black hoody jacket, with a colourful scarf at her throat and several dramatic silver rings on her fingers, because she buys herself one of those after finishing each novel. She was born in Bath in 1945, just as the war ended. Her parents lived in rented rooms in the same house as her grandparents. Her father Harry was a civil servant and her mother Biddy dealt in antiques and they moved to Kingston, just south-west of London, when Jackie was six. 'We got a council flat there,' she says. 'My mother cried, she was so happy to have her own place.'

The pioneering eighteenth-century educator Friedrich Froebel once said: 'Play is the highest expression of human development in childhood, for it alone is an expression of what is in a child's soul.' For Jackie, playing meant making things up.

'When it came to picking teams, everybody would say: "I'll have anybody but Jackie." I couldn't catch a ball, I couldn't throw a ball, I couldn't run fast. And it was pretty humiliating. So it was wonderful I could write stories.'

The Maggots won her praise at school, but another story won her a way to escape. The publisher DC Thomson was looking for material for a new magazine aimed at teenage girls, so she sent off a piece about going to a posh dance and being the only one not to get off with a boy. It was jokey, warm and empathetic, written to make other girls who had gone through the same agonies laugh a little. As a result, Jackie was offered a job with the company up in Dundee, at the age of seventeen. That was a daring decision, to go there, but this was another way of freeing herself from the turmoil at home.

'I lived in the Church of Scotland Girls' Hostel and for a while they didn't have enough rooms for me, so the matron said: "We're not turning you away, you can live in the linen cupboard." No windows or anything.'

Quite warm though, I should imagine.

'Yes, warm,' she says, nodding. 'The warmest place in the hostel. And it was a good way of making friends, because only the girls' living room had a fire, so upstairs was freezing. So loads of people wanted to be my friend and squeeze in the cupboard with me. They were funny times, but good times.'

There is some debate about whether *Jackie* magazine was named after her – it was a popular name at the time, not least because of the incredibly glamorous but recently bereaved Jackie Kennedy – but there's no doubt *Jackie* became one of the bestselling publications in Britain and ran for decades. Meanwhile the real Jackie, who was still a teenager, met a printer called Millar and married him in 1965, when she was just nineteen. They had a daughter called Emma two years later. Millar became a policeman, the little family moved south and Jackie never gave up on the stories. She made them up for her daughter and in time started to try to write books as well as articles; although, actually, it was a very long time before she had any real success: 1991, in fact.

By that time she was in her forties, a very grown-up woman with a grown-up daughter, but still playful and bursting with imagination. Her breakthrough was *The Story of Tracy Beaker*, based on a stroppy teenager in a care home who longs for a family, much as Jackie had longed for siblings when she wrote *The Maggots* as a child. There were many sequels and a massively popular television series based on the book and when a poll was taken in 2003 to find the hundred most popular books in Britain, her titles were on the list: *Double Act*, *Girls in Love*, *Vicky Angel* and *Tracy Beaker*.

The stories are mainly for children but they include all sorts of difficult subjects like divorce, depression, alcoholism, even abuse. They always have happy endings though, she makes sure of that. 'I do think it helps to see a character going through some of what you are going through, because as a child, you can feel you are unique and that nobody else ever feels the way you do. I'm trying to say: "It's okay. Lots of people go through this. It will get better, because you grow and you get more power and you can choose to do things."'

She really seems to care for those who read her. 'I don't like to pretend everything is wonderful, but I do like there to be hope.'

✳   ✳   ✳

'Let's go for a walk,' she says and so we set off, with Jackie in black Moon Boots picking her way past rabbit holes and brambles. 'If you told me even ten years ago that I would have a big garden and actually a field, I would have said you were completely bonkers,' she says. 'I was very much a townie sort of person, then circumstances changed. My mother, who was very elderly and in need of a lot of care, passed away. And I realised I was actually free to move from Kingston, where I'd lived most of my life, and live anywhere I wanted to.'

We can see all the way down the valley as the shining River Cuckmere snakes away to freedom in the sea. 'The Channel is about two miles away,' she says, 'but it does look close. So it's lovely just to open the curtains in the morning and see the sea.' For a writer who can spend a lot of time indoors, this must be a good thing. 'You can be stuck over a piece of work, but going for a good long tramp somewhere near to home is the way of solving everything.'

Great, I say, stumbling over a rabbit hole, but we don't all have our own field.

'No. Mind you, it's a good job we're all into rewilding now,' she says. 'There are anthills, there are so many badgers, there are rabbits and little rodents and amazing insects; it's really got everything. It hasn't actually been properly cultivated for many years. So it's going to take some work.' She pauses for breath and smiles. 'And, well, my job is just to admire and walk here. My partner's job is to get her strimmer and get cracking. She enjoys it. I enjoy it. The dog enjoys it too.'

There is an idea called Deep England which speaks to something essential, rural, idyllic about the English country-side; which harks back to the illusion of a simpler, greener, quieter, happier time and could be said to be profoundly conservative but also feeds the poetry of Thomas Hardy, the painting of John Constable and the ascending lark of Vaughan Williams; and it seems to live here in this valley, with the meandering river, the rising downland and the distant, pretty cottages; but there's something even deeper and darker in the crow-filled trees, the chalk symbols of a horse and a giant found on nearby hills, the hidden, ancient burial sites and the drift of the clouds as evening falls.

'You also see the worrying side of things here,' she says. Just recently, somebody has been setting alight the hay bales, destroying the winter feed for local farmers. 'The police are pretty certain it's arson: not just idiots mucking about but an organised thing, and that's very worrying.' Why would someone do that? 'I have no idea. I do wonder if it's people who are anti-farming?' These are cattle farms. There are sheep too. Animals kept for the killing and the eating. 'So, it's not idyllic. Human nature is human nature. But it's still got its magic, and its connections with the past.'

History lies visible in this landscape, with Bronze Age settlements evident in the rise and fall of the fields and a yew tree nearby that first began to grow when the Romans were in charge. 'You can't help but feel some kind of connection to the place as it was and the people who lived here before.'

There is a kind of enchantment about the place, I say.

'It is fantastic. The chalk horse on the hill is lovely.'

Nobody is really quite sure why the figure of a prancing white horse was cut in chalk on the side of the hill above the river. Some say it was put there as a prank by farm boys in Victorian times; others that it is a tribute to a lost love who fell from just such a horse. It's a beautiful, mysterious thing anyway. And hidden away from us in the distance, just over Windover Hill, is the Long Man of Wilmington: a huge white outline of a figure holding two long poles, who looks more like a woman to me; and it looks like a massive crime scene drawing, but nobody knows if it is a fertility symbol, a sacred sign or even a giant piece of graffiti from the English Civil War, which divided families around here and caused villages to oppose their near neighbours. 'When you come out to walk the dog at night, the stars are just incredible,' she says. 'Even the moon seems much more beautiful from this angle. And of course we get lovely sunrises and sunsets too.'

The wistful way she talks about it makes me wonder: is there a spiritual dimension to this for her? 'I think there has to be, but not in a specific, deliberate way. It's hard not to look up at the stars and feel almost reassured by your insignificance, compared to all of this. And just occasionally you get that sudden burst of joy, in a way, for what you see.'

The sudden surge of feeling connected to nature and all around you is an experience common to humans across times and cultures, as we have already explored together in this book, particularly in the company of Seamus Heaney, Philip Pullman and the kestrel, which I tell Jackie about now. 'I'm not a religious person, but a view can move me, a beautiful painting can move me,' she says. 'I love walking around old churches.'

There's a stunning one not far from here: the tiny church at Lullington, where no more than a dozen people can sit or stand at any time and where – on a warm, still day like this one, when the door is open – the birdsong and the breeze and the insects and the spirit of the land come drifting in. 'The fact that people have been finding comfort or praying there for centuries, or just looking at the paintings, gives you a sense of continuity that is comforting,' she says. 'We're not alone.'

It's touching, how content she seems here, tucked away. 'I was quite happy living in a small terraced house for many years, with so many books you were in danger of them falling on you the moment you stepped in the hallway.'

I've heard she had fifteen thousand? 'Yes, but after a while I did think it would be nice to have a lot of space,' she says. 'So this is not a house beautiful, it's not a listed house, but it's a comfy house. We can spread ourselves.'

Then Jacqueline Wilson says: 'Upstairs, I've got rather strange rooms.'

Okay. What does she mean?

'I've got a kind of nursery room which has lots of fairy-tale books in it and different bits and pieces. This is a house to indulge myself in.' A nursery room? 'Yes. With dolls and toys and many books. I do collect books. Although I don't write fairy tales, I am rather attracted to them. So I have a whole selection.'

Therapists often say we should connect with our younger selves for the sake of healing, so is that what Jackie is doing in that room? 'Well, not consciously, but it makes sense. I had an odd childhood. My parents didn't get on. I don't sit there playing with Barbie dolls or anything but there are toys, mostly older toys. I do like to have things like that around me. I suppose, partly, they are the sort of things I might have loved as a child.'

She says this with disarming honesty, but then again, playfulness is the source of her creativity. Without it there would be no books. When Jackie had her daughter she was only twenty-one years old herself and she loved to get down on her knees and play.

'If she wanted me to play some elaborate imaginary game, that was sheer bliss for me,' she says. 'I think it's good to still have a bit of a child within you. I think it's good to connect with your inner child.'

*   *   *

'Jackson! Come on!' A voice calls out and a dog comes bounding past, half Patterdale, half poodle, a rescue from Battersea Dogs Home and a whippersnapper compared to their elderly cat Jacob. The voice belongs to Jackie's partner, Trish. Finding her was a late revelation in life: Jacqueline and Millar Wilson had been married for more than thirty years, not all of them wildly happy, when the marriage broke down. Jackie was single and content for a while, then like a scene from one of her books, lightning struck. On a weekend away she met a bookseller called Trish and felt a strong sense of attraction, suddenly and to her own great surprise; and being at a stage of life where she was able just to see where it went and be playful, Jackie called up the bookshop where Trish worked and asked for her address, so she could write a letter. It said she had enjoyed their meeting and would love to do an event together, although there was a little more at stake than that.

'I surprised myself,' says Jackie. 'I've always been quite open-minded but I hadn't considered the possibility of actually having a gay relationship. But I thought: this is interesting . . .' Unexpected too, presumably? 'Certainly was. I certainly wasn't a repressed person and I had a long marriage then I was six years on my own and although it got lonely sometimes it was good for me to learn how to be independent, because my daughter had long since left home. This is the interesting thing: you can meet somebody and you just click and that's that, and to me, it doesn't really matter whether they're male or female, because it's personality that matters.' She reflects for a moment, hands clasped. 'The one thing getting older teaches you is: if this happens, don't stand back. Don't let it go. Go for it and that's that.' It's not just age that has given her this attitude. Jackie has been through two life-threatening illnesses in recent years: heart failure and kidney failure and a kidney transplant. Trish actually donated a kidney to someone else, so that they could do a swap and save two lives, including Jackie's. Now that's love.

'Well, it is, isn't it?' She grins. 'Which makes it quite hard to be really cross with her if she's annoying me, but there we go.'

I suddenly feel the urge to tell her about one of my daughters, who grew up on her stories and is now nineteen and part of that generation that has rewritten the rules so that gender is less important than connection: if you love someone, you love someone – and it might be a certain kind of someone today, another kind of someone in the future. That's incredibly refreshing, I say. 'Yes,' says Jackie. 'I mean, being practical, you get more choice too!'

* * *

We're back inside the house now, sitting together in the wood-panelled dining room with tea, talking about how Jackie and Trish went to Vermont in 2008 and married in the grounds of a Victorian hotel with a pair of friends as witnesses. She didn't say publicly that she was in a relationship with another woman until twelve years later, by which time those health challenges had brought her a new boldness.

'I'd always prided myself on being almost superhuman. I could sign books for hour after hour and have a lot of energy. Then suddenly life changes dramatically.'

Theoretically, she now feels like someone on borrowed time: as a survivor of serious illness, but also because she has found her father's death certificate and discovered that he suffered from the same two specific problems: failure of the heart and kidney.

'Modern medicine and skilled people and a bit of luck have actually given me all this extra time. It has made me feel more like: "Seize the day, do everything you want to do, and be joyful about it."'

* * *

I really don't mean to be rude, but after a couple of scares and at the age of seventy-six, has she thought about what comes next? Jackie's eyes shine in response to the question.

'Trish's mother died and she wanted to see her in her coffin,' she says quietly and carefully. 'We could see quite clearly that although she was exactly the same woman, she also wasn't that woman at all. I found it comforting. I hope Trish did too, because you could see that her spirit, if we call it that, was not there at all.' What's she hoping for herself? 'I rather have a hope that I might be cremated and put in a very decorative pot on a bookshelf somewhere out of the way.' She becomes thoughtful. 'Once Trish's gone I think it will be down to Emma, my daughter, to scatter me, wherever. But you cling to the idea you can all stay together.' She's talking about some kind of afterlife, where lovers and families are reunited. 'I just don't know,' she says. 'It will be interesting to find out.'

The stories she's told and the effect they have had on people's lives over several generations will take a long time to die out, won't they? 'It's a lovely thought. I would like my books still to be read but I write for today's children. Also, I suppose, for the child I was. I would have liked to read stories like my own.'

Not every child is the same, of course: her daughter Emma hated any story with sadness or conflict so Jackie had to daydream in a different way. 'I had to write her stories about very happy little girls who were allowed to wear pink all the time, and eat whatever they wanted to eat and had this idyllic way of life,' she says. 'Excuse me a moment . . .'

There's a bell ringing. Jackie looks alarmed. It's dark outside. Who could be here at this time?

'Was that you?' says Trish, rushing in.

'No,' says Jackie and they exchange glances, wondering whether to answer. Then Jackie looks down and smiles. 'There's a bell there, under the carpet,' she says to me. 'I think it was your foot.'

This was the dining room in the old days and when the first course had been served the lady of the house would press the bell discreetly and the servants would come in to clear the dishes. What a grand, strange place for a girl and a boy who grew up in a couple of council houses to find ourselves in. I can't resist it. I press the bell again and it's funny, because Trish calls out again from the next room and Jackie pretends to start. And I do it once more: the dog barks and now we're all laughing. It's a lovely shared moment and gets to the heart of things, because what Jacqueline Wilson does is let her imagination run wild and play. This has brought about huge changes in her life, from a council house in Kingston to the gorgeous Cuckmere valley, from loneliness to friendship and family and the kind of popularity she dreamed of; and a love late in life that she never saw coming; and the playing out in real life of the scenario she made up on the way home from school, when she pretended to be interviewed about her books and told herself the story of Jacqueline Wilson the great writer, which has now very much come true.

'A lot of people stick to the social class they were born in,' she says. 'A type of life that's more or less the same as their parents' or their grandparents'. I haven't done that. I've also gone from being a very shy child who really couldn't say boo to a goose, to this.'

She means her public life, of which our conversation is an example, although we're talking in private, in her home, her safe space. Her house of dreams.

'I've had to go out there and give endless talks and meet up with people and put them at their ease and everything because of my books and I've become a very different, much less introverted person. You wouldn't think your personality could change, but it has done, so it's hard to get a grip on myself.'

Perhaps. She seems to me to have that grip, though. She's very good company: confident in herself, but willing to admit doubts and to explore and always, always to be playful. She still has the joy of the little girl discovering she can tell stories and how wonderful it is to be lost in them and to see the effect they can have on other people. The lesson I am learning from her today is that as you grow up and experience the world and learn things and expand your mind, the trick is never to lose sight of that inner child. When she talks, I don't hear smugness or arrogance; I hear surprise and gratitude.

'I knew the way I wanted to be as a child and as a young woman but I wasn't quite there,' she says, with a sense of wonder. 'It isn't as if I've pretended or anything, but I have actually become what I hoped I would be.'

*　　*　　*

Zahra

If you stand on the beach at Calais on a sunny day, the white cliffs of Dover look startlingly close. They shine like a beacon across the waves, white and pure. The distance from here to there is twenty-one miles, but it feels much closer when the sun is out. It is so easy to think that if you got in a small boat now and just paddled and paddled you could make it over the Channel easily. You could get there. On the end wall of a building by the beach is a Banksy mural that shows a small girl with a suitcase looking through a telescope across the sea from here in France to England on the other side. On her shoulder is a vulture, a symbol of death waiting for her to try, because that stretch of water is so deceptive: it's so beautiful and so deadly. I happen to be here with a French fisherman, who says a gale is starting out in the middle of *La Manche*, invisible to us on what seems to be a lovely day. The sea looks calm enough, but when I ask if he will take me across in his fishing boat this morning he laughs and says: '*Non*! That would be suicide.'

So instead I want to tell the story of someone who did make that crossing in a far smaller boat than his; not even a boat really but a tiny rubber dinghy overloaded with people, barely afloat and letting in water, in the middle of winter, arriving as the dawn came on Christmas Day. Her name is Zahra. That's the name she says I can use anyway. She says it means brilliant or shining bright in Farsi, her first language. We've seen how Jacqueline Wilson told her own story into being and remade her life, but in this final chapter I want to introduce you to a young woman who has done the same in the face of some of the most intense challenges imaginable. Her experience takes the things we have been talking about to extremes. Many of the people we have met can be described as icons and that is true of Zahra too: not on her own, but together with the other men and women, boys and girls who have risked their lives to cross the Channel in small boats over the last few years. Icons of all that's wrong with the world, according to some people. Demonised by politicians and characterised as an invading army, which is ridiculous when you actually meet some of them. Let's do that now.

*   *   *

The English summer is thunderous and rain-soaked and Covid stalks us all, but in Folkestone there's shelter and warmth and good food and a welcome courtesy of a woman called Bridget who helps run a project to assist those who have come across the water who are too old to be taken into care as children, too young to be regarded as adults. They get a foster family if they're lucky, then later a place in a flat with maybe half a dozen others they don't know, some of them unable to cook or clean or manage British money for themselves, or negotiate life in this new land. Bridget and her volunteers help them. And here's Zahra, looking like any other teenager with her trainers and black jeans, hoodie and nose ring, long black hair extensions and painted nails, but her story is astonishing.

I know you think you've heard it before. I thought I had too, but I was wrong, there is far more to it than I realised and it resonates deep inside, for reasons that are very old. It is certainly as inspiring as anything else in this book, maybe even more so. This is the summer of 2020 and I've just been to see the movie *1917*, set in the trenches of the First World

War but based on an ancient kind of story: the epic quest, in which the hero or heroine has to leave their home and strike out for safety, or something that will save their community. They cross the threshold into another world, feel themselves lost like Jonah in the belly of a whale, then go on a journey overcoming huge obstacles, negotiating confusing situations, striking alliances, fleeing dangerous strangers, resisting tricksters, defeating monsters, finding new strength they didn't know they had, confronting their greatest fears, risking their life again and again to travel far, facing a moment when everything seems lost, all is despair and still they rise. Overcome. Survive. Thrive. Maybe one day they return home or find a new hope. I use those words because *Star Wars* is based on this. *Moby Dick* and *Jane Eyre* and so many other stories going all the way back to the beginnings of human history and belief and storytelling, it's deep inside us. As I sit listening to Zahra with the memory of *1917* in my mind I realise that what she is telling me is more epic and more like an ancient folk tale than anything I saw on screen and this is real. This is her life.

✳   ✳   ✳

There was once a girl who fled her home in wartime, with her father and mother and her family, never looking back, knowing it was dangerous to do so, because her dad had worked for those who'd lost power; only as a postman, but still, that was enough for a death sentence. Life was a struggle in the new land, where they weren't really welcome; but love persists in the least promising places, like flowers blooming in the desert. So as the girl who had fled with her family became a young woman, the world being what it is, she met a boy who was becoming a young man. He was good with his hands, he worked the soil and knew how to make things grow, so he found work as a gardener, nurturing life there in the city. They married and after a while life grew inside the woman too: boys and girls, one of them called Zahra. She grew up in exile among a million other people from Afghanistan who had been forced to live in Iran, perhaps 2 million, maybe more, all cut off from home. Zahra was born and grew up in Tehran and tells me: 'We were not allowed to go to school, we were not allowed to go to work, you just had to live as an illegal person. All the Afghan people, refugees.' She watched planes make trails across the blue sky and wondered what it would be like to fly. Up there, above it all. Free to move, to swoop and soar. Down on the ground, Zahra listened to very old stories told by her mother at bedtime as her head was stroked; but they were tales of a place she had never been, to which her mother said they could never return. The tug of home and the dream of flight couldn't take her there; but neither could she stay forever.

Zahra's father died when she was thirteen, leaving her mother alone with the children. Their difficult situation became even worse, she tells me. 'They were deporting Afghan people to Afghanistan. They said: "You have to go back." My mum said: "We can't go there." She was afraid they would kill us all.' So Zahra and her mother set off to try and make it to somewhere else. A faraway land, a place of promise, where they could be in peace, maybe even belong, at last. At the time, that place was called Germany. Angela Merkel had opened the borders, saying: 'Yes, come here if you're troubled.'

They sought advice. In every story there are allies and helpers but they're not always straight. They're not always good. Sometimes their status is complicated, like the agent they paid to get them to the border with Turkey, before crossing over the long way. 'We walked over the mountains,' she says, as if it was nothing. Those agents lurk all along the way, hustling for money on the coast of Turkey, offering to help Zahra and her mother get across the first great physical barrier they faced after the mountains: the Aegean, the wine-dark sea of Homer's *Odyssey*, the water upon which Jason and the Argonauts sailed and above which Icarus flew, before the sun melted his wings. The name comes from the Homeric verb 'to jump', because an ancient king is said to have jumped from cliffs along these shores. For Zahra, this moment was a leap into the abyss.

It was 2016, the year after the world had been shocked by a photograph of the body of a two-year-old boy washed up on the shoreline: Alan Khurdi, from Syria. His mother and brother also drowned. Hundreds of others had died trying to make the same crossing too by the time Zahra found herself there, such a long way from anything she might have called home. The safe passage they paid for was not what they were given. An eyewitness in the camps along the coast said at the time: 'You can hear the screams of people being forced onto these boats, often using tremendous violence. The smugglers are armed, they have cattle prods, they put the people on the boat and then they tell one of the refugees to steer the boat, often in complete darkness. Many boats end up in trouble, all the time.'

Zahra and her mother crossed in a dinghy meant for a dozen people. It was carrying three dozen, maybe more. Zahra was terrified, soaked through, cold and exhausted, but they made it to the other side, to the island of Lesbos, where the woman and the girl found themselves in a camp among many displaced people, all of them now completely detached from the lives they'd known. This is the place that Susan Sarandon visited as a campaigner, if you remember the story she told about the impact it had on her and how hard it was to deal with, even for a wealthy Hollywood star who was just visiting, trying to help. Zahra and her mother had no choice but to be there. The camp was ferociously hot in summer and freezing cold in winter. Even in the spring, when the blossoms came, it was dangerous. Zahra was young. Men circled her like wolves. They wanted to take her, possess her. Zahra's mother was terrified of that. She turned it over in her mind many times, thinking: 'What can I do to help my daughter escape?'

Zahra knew what she was thinking. 'It was not a safe place for a young lady,' she says, flatly and formally, with the language and the accent of somebody who has spoken a little English all her life but is only just now learning how it all fits together. She was fifteen then and looking for a way out, but as the year turned and the sun grew hot again, Germany all but closed its doors. The Promised Land locked the gates with a sign saying: No Entry. That was a kick in the gut, she says. The end of a dream.

Zahra and her mother were lost, suspended between the old life and a new one that was now impossible, like millions of people in camps around the world, swallowed up like Jonah in the belly of that whale. Their fingerprints were taken and they were warned against leaving: 'If you go to another European country, they will send you back.'

There were, however, rumours of another way. Another place, an exception to the rule, no longer part of Europe, no longer bound to those restrictions, where it was said you could apply for asylum without being turned away: 'Britain, England, they will help you there.' There was nothing left to lose. Zahra's mum decided it was worth separating and risking everything to try and get her daughter to safety. She gathered together as much money as she could, contacting members of her extended family, and gave their last reserves to her daughter to strike out on her own. She held her tight, her face buried in Zahra's neck, and cried and said: 'Be brave, my darling, be brave. Be safe.'

And now the agents step into the story again. A plane to Austria was possible for those with money, one of them said. From there she could take the bus to Paris, to the big terminals. Zahra was soon dizzy from the sights, sounds and smells of the French city, the chaos and the furies and the bodies rushing around her blindly, but she found people outside the station who looked like her and spoke like her and who told her there was a place she could go to for food and a shower and rest, if only for a day or two. Then you had to move on, they said. Nobody was friendly. Some of the men were hostile. Some were scary. Some came close in the night. She sat with her eyes open, until the light grew again.

From Paris, Zahra took the train to Calais, where somebody had told her there were others like her trying to do the same thing, to make it to that new land of hope. It's an old story. You'd do the same, if you needed to flee, if you needed to find a place where you could be safe, where they spoke a language you understood, where you could begin again. You'd risk everything for that chance for you and yours, surely?

Zahra found herself in The Jungle, a notorious camp where hundreds were waiting. She had no contacts. She had no help. 'I was a young woman, I was alone.'

And here they are again: the watchers and the waiters, the helpers of this story, the strangers, the agents, who have been there every step of the way, from Tehran to Turkey to Lesbos to Paris and now here on the shoreline. Hanging around like the wolf in Red Riding Hood, flashing their teeth, offering smooth words, making big promises, ready to swallow up all her money and anything else they can get.

'Oh, Grandma, what a big boat you have.'
'All the better to drown you in, my love.'

*   *   *

The cheapest, quickest way to get across was on a lorry, so Zahra and a couple of boys she had never met before were taken down to the lorry park after dark and shown how to run alongside these massive vehicles as they slid past, huge and imposing like beasts in the night. Zahra did it. She somehow summoned up the courage to jump, cling to the back and climb up to join the boys inside. But the driver hit the brakes and there were screaming sounds and a hissing like snakes and the lorry stopped and he was shouting at them: 'Get off, get off, get off!' He looked like he was going to hit them, so they jumped and ran. She was buzzing with the excitement of it, but also cold and angry and scared. And desperate enough to try again the next night.

This time Zahra and the boys managed to stay on, they managed to stay hidden, but one of the boys said: 'No, something's wrong, something's wrong!' He was looking at his phone, watching the location on his app. The signal was bouncing up to a satellite high in space and back down again, telling him the lorry was heading the wrong way: not to the ferries and to England but inland. Now the two boys were banging and banging on the wall of the lorry until the driver heard them. And when he opened the door to see what was going on, they leapt out and ran, back to the camp.

The next day, Zahra felt empty. She thought of the white cliffs shining, looking close enough to touch, but it was twenty-one miles across this last great expanse of sea and she was afraid to go back on the water after the last time. This was further, it was much colder, the weather was worse, it was much scarier, but there didn't seem to be any other way. Enter an agent, cooing in her ear: 'It's okay. Lots of people are doing it. You'll be safe.'

The last of her money went to this man full of promises. 'You'll have food, drink, everything you need on board.' He came in the night with a minibus and took Zahra and some others out of the camp, an hour along the wide French coastal roads, then a few moments on tight lanes. 'Here it is. Here we are.'

The bus had stopped on the gravel by a remote beach, where nobody would see them launch a boat or try to stop them. They all walked towards the waves, but the agent went back for something and the others followed. Zahra was left alone on the beach in the dark, with the wind picking up and the stars bright across the wide canopy of the night sky, falling down into her face. She could smell the sea, taste the salt on her lips again, hear the voice of her mum telling her: 'Be brave, my darling, be brave.'

She wanted her mum so much. Zahra was shaking with the cold or the fear.

The figures came back out of the shadows and they had with them no boat but a big square box. And so it was that the agent unfolded and inflated the craft on which their lives would depend, right there on the beach. He fitted a tiny motor and showed one of the boys how to work it. And he pointed to the red lights across the water, the signal lights of Dover. This was just a boy he was telling, just a child, maybe sixteen years old, the same age as Zahra; but the agent said: 'You're in charge now. Follow the lights.'

Zahra didn't know it was the busiest shipping lane in Europe. She didn't know there were speedboats and yachts and fishing boats darting around like predators, or that there were giant monsters out there, freighter leviathans moving through the waters, stopping for nobody, ready to swallow anything or anyone that got in their way. She didn't know any of that, but she was still scared. Another boy was shouting at the agent: 'Why did you lie to me, why did you lie?' Zahra's face was wet with rain or stinging salt water or tears, she didn't know which. 'I don't want to go,' she cried over the sound of the waves. 'I can't.'

And here it is. The low point of the story. The point of no return. After all those miles, all those risks, all those dangers. Do this. Get there. Or die trying.

The big bad wolf of a smuggler turned to her, eyes burning bright in the night. 'You're not getting your money back.'

Zahra had nothing left. She had nowhere to go. The little rubber boat overloaded with people was swaying in the surf, already unsteady, already unsafe.

She got in.

*   *   *

I wanted to know what it was like out there, so I found myself another fisherman. We set off from Dover at dusk with the wind beginning to howl and the temperature dropping fast. I was dressed properly, in the kind of thermals and wet weather gear refugees seldom have, but I was soon freezing. Six miles out from the English shore, on the edge of the shipping lanes, the engines were turned off and we drifted. I knew I was safe on this modern fishing boat but the inky blackness of the sea suddenly felt overwhelming, a hint of how terrifying it must be to be stuck out here at night in an overloaded rubber dinghy with the water sloshing over the sides into the craft, weighing you down, the waves threatening to overcome. Low in the water with no proper lights or signals, you'd be in serious danger of getting run down by one of the many other vessels. Those freighters are vast, like skyscrapers floating on their sides, but moving fast, completely blind to little rubber boats.

Five red lights in a vertical line dominated the darkness and I took them to be the lights the driver of Zahra's boat was told to aim for. 'You can see that all the way over on the other side, but it is so dangerous what they're doing,' the fisherman told me. 'I'm really surprised people haven't died.' That was true then but it is not now. There have been many deaths and the ones we know about began with a doctoral student from Iran in her thirties called Mitra Mehrad, a young woman full of promise, burning bright with desire to be of use in the world, who jumped over the side of a sinking dinghy and into the water to try to catch a rescue rope, to try to save a baby from drowning. Nine days later, her body washed up among the pillars of a wind farm off the coast of Holland, one hundred miles away. I thought of her as we drifted; and of a boy called Akoy, a friend of Zahra, who had been out here on a dinghy that was sinking. 'I was scooping out the water like this with a bucket for hours,' he had told me when I met him, making a hand motion to show the shifting of the waves. His eyes were wet with tears and the memory of fear. 'The others texted their families to say goodbye. I would have texted my brother, but I didn't have my phone. We were all saying the prayer we say as Muslims when we are going to die.'

They survived, but nobody knows exactly how many others have perished.

'Hang on, we've got company,' said the fisherman as we drifted in silence, having spotted the symbol for a Border Force cutter on his radar. 'They must think we're people smugglers.' The grey that camouflages these large patrol boats during the day must act like stealth paint at night, because all I could see was a black shape, a vast moving shadow and a couple of lights shining at us. That is often how the crossing ends, for the lucky ones.

✻   ✻   ✻

Zahra's boat did not sink. They made it across the sea, the last great obstacle on her 7,000-mile journey, in the early hours of Christmas morning; the beginning of a day when some of us remember the story of another refugee woman who gave birth in exile.

Zahra was sick from the swell, but they reached the beach, where the tide was out. She jumped over the side and onto the sand, unsure what to do, with the dawn just beginning to break around her. One of the boys tried to ring the British police to let them know what was happening and he was asked: 'Where are you?'

The boy could see strange arches and the statue of a mermaid in the half-light, but he had no way to put a name to this. Then suddenly a stranger was marching towards them on the beach, an older man, shouting and taking control: 'Come with me, come with me.'

'We were very cold and very wet,' remembers Zahra, who was still frightened. Her legs were like jelly from the motion of the waves and the worry. The police in France had beaten up her friends. They'd torn down people's shelters and kicked over their stoves. She was terrified of those officers in their dark uniforms who were so full of hatred, who treated them like animals and had made it impossible to think of staying in France. So Zahra braced herself when the officials arrived. She was ready for the worst. But the British police were nice, as it turned out. They had gentle, careful voices. One of them was a woman who said: 'We'll take care of you.' She took them to a building where they were given new clothes instead of their wet ones. And Zahra felt dry; and they were given hot drinks and food and Zahra began to feel strong again. And instead of the battle she'd been expecting, she found a welcome. She was barely ready for it. This was a great surprise.

Zahra was eventually placed with a good foster family, because she was still a child.

'My mum was very worried. She didn't know where I was. The family gave me a phone so I was able to call her.'

I ask her then: 'Is your mum still alive?'

'Yeah,' she says, smiling.

Is she in Greece?

'No, she's in England.'

What? When did she come?

'Last year.'

How did she get here?

'She came in a boat, like me. She didn't tell me. She didn't want to worry me.'

Zahra giggles then explains that one day her mother rang and said, out of the blue: 'I'm in England.' She lives in London but struggles with her nerves. 'Everything makes her very nervous.' Did Mum come all this way on her own? 'Yeah. She's a hero of me.'

A hero of mine. A heroine. I said Zahra was an icon, or that people like her are anyway. Icons usually point us to something bigger, better, a higher path or a better way of being ourselves, and they are also often made in our own image: a Russian image of Jesus looks like a Russian; an Ethiopian Mary has the face of a woman from Addis Ababa. They are Other but they are also us. And that's what I've learned from meeting Zahra and Akoy and others. If we perceived them as being us, not as alien or other, we would tell their lives very differently, like stories not just of suffering or of imposition but of adventure and survival and bravery.

Maybe that's what I'm trying to do now. Zahra wants me to tell the story for her, while she prepares to tell it herself. She laughs when I ask her to take away the baklava that someone at the project has made and is passing round because it's too delicious and I'm going to eat it all. And she smiles, so widely, when she shares some news: 'I was given my refugee status a few days ago.'

'Wow,' says Bridget, sitting beside her. 'That's huge.' And it is. At the age of nineteen, for the first time in her entire life, this young, smart, determined woman who has come so far and overcome so much is living somewhere legally. She was born in exile, but right now Zahra has the right to be somewhere. In the great archetypal stories the hero or the heroine sometimes returns home, but sometimes they can't. And sometimes they discover that home is possible wherever they are, in this new place where they live now. Zahra lives by the sea, learning English, hoping to be useful. She's studying hard and has a dream. To fly. Not just metaphorically or in story terms: she wants to be a pilot.

And there's a twist to this tale, because Bridget, the remarkable woman who helps run the project where I've come to meet Zahra, went on holiday one summer, to a Greek island. It was almost the reverse of the journey Zahra made, but Bridget was a traveller with a wage, a passport and a freedom of movement that made it easy, or would have done if the flights had not been messed up somehow. So she got in a fight with the travel company on social media and the managing director happened to see what she did, and got in touch directly to say: 'Is there anything we can do to help?'

Bridget seized the moment: 'We've got a young refugee here who wants to fly . . .'

The managing director actually paid for a flying lesson for Zahra, and others in the industry did the same at his suggestion. They're looking for an apprentice degree that she can take in time, to work in the aviation industry and maybe one day get her wings.

On a clear summer's morning, a Piper Archer plane took off from Lydd airfield in Kent with a flying instructor at the helm and Zahra by her side. They turned left and followed the coastline, at which point the instructor offered her the chance to fly the plane for a few moments, saying calmly over the intercom: 'You have control.'

The girl who had scrambled ashore on Christmas morning, soaked through and sick to the stomach, confused about where she was and what would happen next, with no sense of control over her life at all, had returned to that same place but now she was seeing it from a different perspective, far above. As high as a bird, higher. She had been driven by hope and now here was joy, as Zahra flew over the beach, through the blue sky of her dreams.

'The view was so good, I loved it so much.'

Some people want to keep her feet on the ground, still.

'The boys laugh and say: "That will never happen. Girls can't be pilots."'

So what does she say to them?

Zahra smiles a shy but determined smile. 'I say: "Just watch me fly."'

*　　*　　*

Acknowledgements

Thank you for reading this book; do please get in touch to let me know what you think. If you happen to feature in one of the stories then thank you so much for the privilege of meeting and writing about you.

Thanks to Rachel, Jacob, Joshua, Ruby and Grace Moreton for all you've taught me about love and family and for putting up with me while these encounters were happening over the years.

Thank you to Andy Lyon at Hodder Faith for believing in this project and seeing it through with patience and grace.

I'm grateful for the wisdom and support of Jessica Foster, theologian and friend, who listened to the raw stories and helped make them wider, deeper and better.

Thanks to David Perry, Emily Jeffery, Paul and Claire Tabraham, Glyn Moreton, Andy Partington, Bruce Pont, Russell Boulter, Nadine Bateman, Malcolm Doney and Martin Wroe for friendship, advice and expertise as the podcast evolved into the book.

Thank you to the families of Clive James and Dame Vera Lynn for supporting the project and to Jacqueline Wilson for a completely new interview.

I would like to thank the editors and colleagues I worked with on the interviews for national newspapers that inspired some of these stories, including Ted Verity, Andrew Davies, James Mannion, Gordon Thomson, Jo Elvin and Geordie Greig at the *Mail* and *Mail on Sunday*; Lisa Markwell, James Hanning and Tristran Davies at the *Independent on Sunday*;

Ian MacGregor, Ross Jones and Paul Clements at the *Telegraph*. Other stories had their origins in radio work with the great producer Jonathan Mayo, for Phil Critchlow's TBI Media; many thanks to you both. The kestrel chapter began as a Pause for Thought with Zoe Ball on Radio 2, produced by Michael Wakelin; thank you for the opportunity to think and share. Thanks to Natalie Jerome for sealing the deal that made the podcast and book possible and to Toby Mundy for subsequently becoming my agent, ally and friend.

Great thanks to Jessica Lacey, Linda DeAngelis, Rhoda Hardie and the team at Hodder Faith for believing in the stories and working so hard to get them out there, you really do make it all happen.

Thanks and love to Mum and Dad, Arthur and Marion, and to my sister Vicki.

And most of all to you, lovely reader of a rare and precious kind, who has somehow made it all the way to the end of this list; your collaboration is the most valuable of all. Thank you so much for your perseverance and kindness. Simone Weil was absolutely right: attention is the purest form of generosity and I am very grateful for yours.